REVENUE MATTERS

Tax the rich
and restore
Democracy
to save the nation

Berkley Bedell

TABLE OF CONTENTS

ACKNOWLEDGEMENTS

This book would not have been written without the help and encouragement of my good friend Jim Frost over the lengthy time we have been working together on it. I have also received help from Rachael Garrity, who has put the book into proper format for printing. Language, encouragement and other suggestions have come from Erica and Ann Stevens; and my friends, Ann Esse, Florence and Leon Hesser, John Limpitlaw, Joanne Quinn, Smith Schuneman, Dr. Merle Otto, Elizabeth Geiser, Klaus-Peter Voss, Cabell Brand, Sam Pizzagati, Jean Gibbs, Bill Van Arsdale, David Caswell, and others.

I also have to thank my wife, Elinor for putting up with the time I have spent on this project and the times when I have not been available to spend time with her doing the things we both like to do.

FINANCIAL WEALTH DISTRIBUTION IN THE UNITED STATES

In terms of types of financial wealth, the top one percent of households have 38.3 percent of all privately held stock, 60.6 percent of financial securities, and 62.4 percent of business equity. The top 10 percent have 80 percent to 90 percent of stocks, bonds, trust funds and business equity, and over 75 percent of non-home real estate. Since financial wealth is what counts as far as the control of income-producing assets, we can say that just 10 percent of the people own the United States of America.

~ Professor William G. Domhoff, *Wealth, Income and Power*

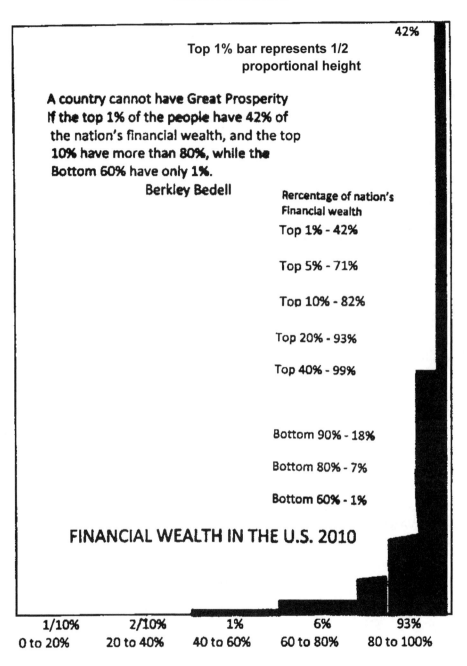

42%

Top 1% bar represents 1/2
proportional height

A country cannot have Great Prosperity
If the top 1% of the people have 42% of
the nation's financial wealth, and the top
10% have more than 80%, while the
Bottom 60% have only 1%.

Berkley Bedell

Percentage of nation's
Financial wealth

Top 1% - 42%

Top 5% - 71%

Top 10% - 82%

Top 20% - 93%

Top 40% - 99%

Bottom 90% - 18%

Bottom 80% - 7%

Bottom 60% - 1%

FINANCIAL WEALTH IN THE U.S. 2010

| 1/10% | 2/10% | 1% | 6% | 93% |
| 0 to 20% | 20 to 40% | 40 to 60% | 60 to 80% | 80 to 100% |

Chart based on statistics reported in *Wealth, Income and Power* by G. William Dornhoff, published originally in 2005 and updated in January 2011. Used by permission.

Show me a business that ignores REVENUE and focuses only on CUTTING COSTS, and I will show you a business that is headed for failure.

Show me a government that ignores REVENUE and focuses only on CUTTING COSTS, and I will show you a government that is a failure.

Show me a business that only CUTS BACK and does not CHARGE FORWARD, and I will show you a business that is headed for failure.

Show me a government that only CUTS BACK and does not CHARGE FORWARD, and I will show you a government that is a failure.

Berkley Bedell

FROM BOTH SIDES OF THE AISLE

When Berkley Bedell retired from Congress in 1986, he received letters thanking him for his service from more than 150 members of Congress. Below are excerpts from a selection of those letters.

"You have been an articulate idealist and open to suggestions of others. I have appreciated your leadership in the Prayer Breakfast movement and the occasions when we have enjoyed breakfast together. "
~ Richard Lugar, Republican U.S. Senator, Indiana

"Berk was soon recognized as the conscience of our class — indeed, of the whole House of Representatives. His colleagues did observe, however, a serious fault in his conduct as a Congressman — he was straight forward and truthful. Sometimes this was a source of embarrassment to others in public office who were more accustomed to evasiveness and duplicity."
~ Father Robert Cornell, Democratic Congressman, Wisconsin

"It has been a truly great experience to work with you as we attempted to solve the problems of our folks back in Iowa as well as those facing the nation as a whole."
~ Cooper Evans, Republican Congressman, Iowa

"It was not only a pleasure, but an inspiration serving with you in Congress. When others were silent, you spoke up. When others were indifferent you cared. When others were nowhere to be found, you were actively promoting the causes in which we both believe. I will never forget your good work."
~ Stephen Solarz, Democratic Congressman, New York

"Regardless of the problems we faced, you were always optimistic and willing to work to the last minute to find the compromise. We have correctly labeled you the conscience of the House Agriculture Committee."

~ Pat Roberts, Republican Congressman, Kansas

"Never have I seen such a man of decency and integrity grace the halls of Congress as you... To you there were no in-betweens on anything. Now that you are O, K. get your ass back here in the House where you belong. Sorry to be so blunt, Berk, but we need you."

~ Bill Richardson, Democratic Congressman, New Mexico

"During the years we have worked together, I came to know not just your professionalism and die-hard work ethic, but also your insight, character and compassion. Your direction helped this great nation grow at the grass roots level and made a tremendous contribution to the nation's future."

~ Silvio Conte, Republican Congressman, Massachusetts

"Your dedication to the survival of the planet and fearless chasing of Pentagon waste was unmatched."

~ Pat Schroeder, Democratic Congresswoman from Colorado

"We had the opportunity to fight many battles together on the Small Business Committee and on the legislation to provide a better life for our farmers. I consider myself fortunate that we were frequently on the same side, because you were a tough adversary. You may be assured that you go with the respect of all who were privileged to serve with you — on both sides of the aisle."

~ Toby Roth, Republican Congressman from Wisconsin

"Personally, politically, officially and in every other relevant way you've been a class act—jointly and singly as we lawyers say. When young people ask me if it's possible to be an effective politician and retain your integrity and dignity, I've always cited Berk as an example. I still will."

~ Barney Frank, Democratic
Congressman from Massachusetts

"What impresses me the most about you is the high standard of personal conduct you set in everything you did here in Washington. I knew I could disagree with you (as I often did) but I always knew that whatever you did came from the heart, and it came along with the highest standards."

~ Bill Frenzel, Republican
Congressman from Minnesota

"You are an extra-ordinarily fine Human being and a great legislator—two traits which often do not go together. You have enriched this country with your service, and have enriched your colleagues with a heart that is as big as the State of Iowa and a commitment to justice and fairness unparalled in the House."

~ Dan Glickman, Democratic
Congressman from Kansas

INTRODUCTION

Recognizing that REVENUE MATTERS,
together we can turn our nation around.

Today I believe we have too many politicians telling us what we can't do. They tell us that we can't continue Social Security at the current level. We can't continue Medicare. We can't tax the rich to reduce the deficit. Don't tell me what we can't do. This book is my effort to tell you what I believe we can do.

It is time for America to wake up. There is a war going on and it is right here in our own country. One side is well organized, powerful and winning. The other side is confused and does not recognize what is happening. Like most wars it is devastating to both sides and the nation. Like most wars, it could be ended tomorrow. It is time for America to wake up--end the war and CHARGE FORWARD.

The war is between the wealthy top 10 percent of the people and the bottom 90 percent. Government policies during recent years of constant tax cuts to the rich has enabled that top 10 percent to now own 82% of the nation's financial wealth (wealth not counting home and contents) leaving only 18%, for the entire rest of our people. That 10% have taken over our federal and state governments and even our Supreme Court with their lobbyists and political contributions; while the people sit helplessly by and sometimes even join their wealthy enemies as they are tricked into believing the propaganda of the wealthy 10 percent.

The 10% furnish almost all of the campaign funds of the politicians either directly or through the corporations and organizations, which they control with their money. With their ownership of the stocks of most corporations, and their positions on Boards of Directors, the 10% pretty well control the national media, either through their advertising dollars, or outright ownership. And we have a Republican House of Representatives that recently tried to end funding of public broadcasting-one media outlet not owned or controlled by corporate interests.

CUT GOVERNMENT SPENDING!! CUT TAXES FOR THE RICH AND CUT GOVERNMENT PROGRAMS FOR THE PEOPLE TO ELIMINATE THE DEFICIT!

This is the cry of the rich and their Republican friends.

I started a fishing tackle manufacturing business, Berkley and Company, with $50 saved from my newspaper route when I was 15 years old. Half of my $50 was spent on a little one inch ad in Spots Afield magazine. From the very beginning I recognized the importance of revenue by investing half my resources to get sales and revenue. From the very beginning, I charged forward.

We continued to charge forward and focus on revenue until I hired a President to run the company and went off to serve in the United States Congress. The new President focused on cutting costs. He cut back on benefits to employees; cut back on advertising, research and marketing. Sales declined, as did revenue and the company was headed for bankruptcy. My son, Tom, came back to run the company and replace the cost cutting President. Tom borrowed all the money he could. He cared about the employees; increased advertising, marketing and research. He focused on revenue and charged forward. When Tom sold the company some time ago, Berkley was by far the largest and most successful fishing tackle manufacturing company in the nation.

Show me a business that ignores revenue and focuses only on cutting costs and I will show you a business that is headed for failure.

Show me a government that ignores revenue and focuses only on cutting costs and I will show you a government that is a failure.

Show me a business that only cuts back and does not charge forward and I will show you a business that is headed for failure.

Show me a government that only cuts back and does not charge forward and I will show you a government that is a failure.

A COST CUTTING, CUT BACK GOVERNMENT IS EXACTLY WHAT THE TEA PARTY REPUBLICANS DEMAND THAT WE HAVE IN THESE GREAT UNITED STATES OF AMERICA AS THIS IS WRITTEN.

In the meantime, we will stand by and watch as foreign nations in which governments work for the people prosper and the people thrive.

We need to send our federal legislators to business school, particularly the Tea Party influenced cut back Republicans. President Obama seems to get it as he fights with the Republicans by trying to raise taxes of the rich and maintain critical programs for the people--but there sure are plenty of Democrats as well as Republicans that could use some time at a business school.

Today our legislators are acting like the father who cannot afford to send his child to college because he did not have the courage to ask his boss for a raise, which the boss would have been glad to give. If the government will just have the courage to tax us according to our ability to pay, there is no limit to what we CAN DO.

I am fortunate. I lived during the middle of the last century, before our current nightmare--the period that Robert Reich, Secretary of Labor in the administration of Bill Clinton calls the "Great Prosperity". Back then, we had a CAN DO government that recognized that REVENUE MATTERS. The top income tax rate fluctuated between 91 and 70 percent. Even with deductions, it was roughly double today's top 35% rate. The nation's wealthiest 1% earned less than 9% of the nation's income. Today they earn 24%.

At the end of World War II, the national debt equaled almost 120% of the country's annual economy, compared to today's roughly 100%. But we did not obsess about trying to balance the budget. We CHARGED FORWARD doing the things that needed to be done to build a better nation--just as Berkley and Company did when it found itself in financial trouble.

Social Security, Medicare and Medicaid dropped the poverty rate of elderly persons by 50%. A 40 hour workweek was established with time and a half paid for overtime. A minimum wage was enacted.

The government passed laws and instituted regulations that increased the power of labor unions. By the mid-50s almost a third of all workers were unionized. Those labor unions demanded a fair share of company profits and higher wages kept America's economic machine going by giving average workers the money to buy what they produced.

Pay for the workers in the bottom fifth of our economy more than doubled. Productivity increased and the median income in 2007 dollars rose from about $25,000 to $55,000 during the period. It showed what we can do with a government that cares about the people and is not controlled by the political contributions of the wealthy and Corporate America.

Today people being hired by Ford Motor Company are paid about half what their grandparents received, in comparable dollars, during the period of Great Prosperity. And today some of those elected to government by the plutocrats and their Tea Party Republicans are trying to destroy the ability of workers to organize and demand decent wages. What a disaster--not just for the workers, but for our whole nation!

We can argue about global warming, but the pollution of our atmosphere, land and oceans is a fact. Our increasing dependence on imported oil is a fact. The reality that the wealthy in America have plenty of money to enable us to convert to clean domestic energy is a fact. Our unemployed who would like to be working is a fact. It is time for us to tax the polluters and the wealthy in our society to put our unemployed to work making ourselves self sufficient with clean energy and restoring our crumbling infrastructure.

A Republican House of Representatives that refuses to let tax cuts to the wealthy expire and votes to bar the government from shutting down mountaintop mines is a legislative body representing polluters without regard to the type of planet we leave to those that follow us. For that same legislative body to vote to prohibit the Environmental Protection Agency from imposing regulations curbing emissions of gasses that pollute our planet is a government representing Corporate America and not the people--or the future of our nation.

When I first started to write this book, I wanted to keep it non-partisan. As a Democrat raised in a Republican family; having served an overwhelmingly Republican district in Congress; as a part of the wealthy 10% and living in an overwhelmingly Republican wealthy retirement community, the easy thing for me to do was to either keep quiet, or write a non-partisan book.

All through my life I have tried to live a comparatively non-partisan life. When I was Chairman of a Small Business Committee in Congress, I traveled to the home areas of Republican members to hold hearings, just as I did for Democrats. While in Congress, I made campaign ads for a Republican member of Congress endorsing him and Republican members of Congress did the same for me.

When I retired from Congress I had more Republicans than Democrats come to the floor of Congress to say nice things about me.

I have always thought that more can be accomplished when people work together, rather than fight each other.

BUT TODAY'S TEA PARTY REPUBLICANS ARE REJECTING COOPERATION AS AN OPTION!

Corporate America and the wealthy have taken over the country and the current Tea Party Republicans are serving as their army. When the Republicans in Congress voted in lock step against repeal of Bush's tax cuts for the wealthy, while proposing cuts in education, pollution control, Medicare and Social Security, I decided I could no longer remain silent. I completely rewrote this introduction.

Situations change. People change. Governments change. And Political Parties change. This book includes a speech by Republican President Theodore Roosevelt. It was Republican President Dwight Eisenhower that warned us of the dangers of a military industrial complex, and under his administration the top tax rate was 91%. I believe they would both be turning over in their graves if they knew what the current Tea Party Republicans are trying to do to our nation.

There are two kinds of people. There are two kinds of businesses. There are two kinds of government. There are those who cut back and there are those who charge forward. You can never get to where you want to go by cutting back. You only get there by charging forward! This book is my effort to alert the people--all of us, that we cannot get out of the mess our country is in today by cutting back. We can only bring back the Great Prosperity by charging forward.

Today the Republicans tell us we can't get sufficient revenue from the wealthy to do what I propose by simply taxing me and the rest of the wealthy. They are partly correct. We need to do more than just tax the wealthy. We need to use the revenue to work with Corporate America to put our people to work replacing our imported oil with clean domestic energy and rebuilding our crumbling infrastructure, while we end the tax loopholes that enable some of our major corporations to completely avoid paying taxes. As our people go back to work, the taxes they pay will reduce the deficit.

But don't tell me what we can't do. That is what people have been telling me all my life. Thank God I did not listen when our local hardware store owner told me that I could not possibly compete with the big fishing tackle manufacturers when as a high school student I started my fishing tackle manufacturing business with $50 from my newspaper route--or when the pollster told me, "Don't run. You do not have a chance" in regard to my running for Congress. Or when one of our salesmen said I must be out of my mind to try to compete with the DuPont Company. I have spent much of my life doing what people tell me can't be done. It has been fun - and it has worked. As a nation we can charge forward as we did at one time--or we can sit on our hands and talk about what we can't do.

I am sure many people, like my hardware store owner, would tell me that it is foolish to try to get the people to rise up against the rich and powerful and Corporate America with all their money and influence and get the people to take back the government. I only know one thing; we can't do it unless we try. It is time for those of us who care about our nation to charge forward and recruit all the others who would like to see a government that serves all the people to rise up and especially to vote and bring our non-voting friends with us.

There will be all kinds of efforts to divert our attention from this overriding issue. There will be an effort to distract us by making abortion, homosexuality, or where Obama was born the issue. There are already efforts to sell false economic theories. We cannot be distracted and the time is now. The longer we let Corporate America and the wealthy 10% own our government, the harder it will be to dislodge them.

Two things are obvious. Either we all continue to sit back and let Corporate America, the wealthy and their Republican friends in Congress demand that we CUT BACK the services to the people as they gather more and more of the nation's wealth into fewer and fewer hands.

Or we can learn from the Tea Party movement. We need to organize and demand a change.

So our workers can sit back and watch as their jobs disappear and their power of collective bargaining declines. Our teachers can watch funding for education be reduced while we cut taxes for the wealthy. Students can watch as funding for education and student grants are cut and job opportunities upon graduation are reduced. And Senior citizens can stand by while legislators would rather cut Social Security than make the rich pay the same rate of Social Security taxes as common workers.

I call upon the workers, both employed and laid off; the teachers whose funds are being cut and whose jobs are in danger; the students whose financial aid is being cut and whose job opportunities upon graduation are disappearing; those of us who care about the environment and the planet we leave to our grandchildren; all of us, including those wealthy that care about our nation; to learn from the Tea Party movement.

WE NEED TO ORGANIZE A "TOGETHER WE CAN MOVEMENT."

A union movement, a teacher movement, and an environment movement are great, but they will not get anywhere until we recognize the common problem, unite and organize. Until we sufficiently tax ourselves to get the REVENUE needed and CHARGE FORWARD to build a nation similar to what we had during the Great Prosperity, the political contributions of the wealthy will continue to rule our nation and destroy the prosperity of the people.

My wife and I are part of that wealthy 10 percent. By turning my newspaper route earnings into a successful business I am a hero in my home town, Bill Gates and Warren Buffet are national heroes. We are not bad people.

It is the system and the government that is all screwed up!

Once we organize a TOGETHER WE CAN movement, we may be surprised at how many of the wealthy will join in the movement. My wife and I are two of them.

People all over the world are rising up in anger over the actions of their government. Fortunately we still have a democracy where votes can be a substitute for violence. Corporate America and the wealthy may have the money, but we have the numbers of voters.

More than one third of our voters do not bother to vote. If we start to seriously demand that we kick out the can't do cut back, Tea Party Republicans, and demand that the Democrats start to charge forward and fight for the people, we may be surprised at how many of those non-voters will join us.

I hope my Republican friends will read this book with an open mind. Nothing could be better than for them to read Theodore Roosevelt's speech and decide to become an old time Republican like Theodore Roosevelt--and like those Republicans with whom I served only a short time ago. I hope they decide they want to charge forward instead of cutting back to bring back the "Great Prosperity" of the past.

In a democracy, it is up to us. Don't let anyone tell us that we CAN'T do it. Shout back, "TOGETHER WE CAN take back our nation."

Chapter 1

MY LIFE AND MY PERSPECTIVE

*TOGETHER WE CAN get back to the Great Prosperity
that existed in my earlier years*

In my 90 years of life I have seen how cooperation and proper distribution of income and wealth can result in a period of Great Prosperity.

I was born into a fishing family. When I was 5 years old, my parents left me on the lake shore with a cane pole and worm on a hook, while they went down the shore with their hip boots and fly rods. Alone there on the shore I pulled in my first fish. My father paraded me all over town to show me off with my fish. I was hooked for the rest of my life.

With my first fish. 1926

As a boy I learned to tie fishing flies from my dog's tail, similar to the ones my parents used. When I was 15 years old, and a sophomore in High School, I convinced my parents that I should be permitted to take $50 I had saved from my newspaper route and start my own business of making and selling my fishing flies.

With the $50 I purchased the needed hooks, hair, feathers and thread, and had a little 6 page catalog printed showing the flies I had to sell. I spent nearly half my $50 on a one page ad in Sports Afield magazine promoting sales of Berkley's flies. From the very beginning, my focus was on sales and REVENUE.

By the time I graduated from High School, I had three girls working for me in their home making flies and fishing leaders. A fishing leader is the item that goes between the fishing line and the hook or lure to keep the fish from biting through the line.

Upon graduating from High school, I again convinced my parents that I should be permitted to see if I could build this business into a major success. The only area that I felt gave me the opportunity I wanted was to make cable wire fishing leaders. Unfortunately I did not know how to make them.

At that time the major fishing tackle distributers printed their catalogs and did their buying in the fall of the year for the next season. Unless you could obtain their orders in the fall, there was no point in calling on them until the next fall.

I worked really hard all summer. I could make samples, but I could not figure out how to make these wire fishing leaders in a production process.

Berkley Fishing Tackle Factory in my bedroom, which I shared with my brother Jack. 1936

I did not let that stop me. I printed a price list with prices just 10% lower than the lowest price anyone charged for wire fishing leaders and made a sample book of the leaders I proposed to sell. I removed the right hand front seat of my parents' only car, and built a bed on the right side of the car. I started off on a trip calling on large wholesale hardware and fishing tackle distributors to sell these wire fishing leaders that I did not know how to make in a motor home that was ahead of its time.

I went up through Minnesota to Duluth, down through Wisconsin, through Illinois, Michigan, Indiana and Ohio. When I arrived in Louisville, Kentucky, there was a telegram waiting for me. HURRY HOME STOP. THERE ARE TOO MANY ORDERS WE DO NOT KNOW HOW TO MAKE. STOP.

On the way home I stopped in South Bend, Indiana, the home of the major wire fishing leader manufacturer. I scurried around the town and found the machine shop that made their equipment, which turned out to be a simple little solder pot with a spout and a slot in the top of the spout in which you could dip the wire to solder the joint.

I was gone for three weeks; travelled over 3,000 miles; and spent less than $50 for the entire trip - for 20 cent per gallon gasoline, 5 cent milk and 5 cent bread--and with no cost for lodging.

Returning, I took my orders to the local bank, whose Board consisted of parents of my school buddies. They loaned me the money I needed to buy the supplies and pay the workers, and Berkley Fishing Tackle Company was a reality.

**The entire staff of Berkley and Company in 1940.
My brother Jack is second from the right. The three youth between
the Bedell brothers were all members of my
1939 High School graduating class.**

It was not surprising that I could make a profit selling leaders for 10 percent less than anyone else. My home was my factory. I had no rent, no overhead, and I paid my school buddies 15 cents per hour, which they were glad to get.

Berkley and Company continued to grow as we moved out of my parent's house to uptown facilities and CHARGED FORWARD.

That beginning set the stage for my business career. The message is sell, charge forward and REVENUE MATTERS.

My Grandmother had a saying, "You can do almost anything within reason if you will only put your mind to it." I "put my mind" to charging forward with my business, and I never looked back.

It is time for our government to do as I did in business; recognize that REVENUE MATTERS and charge forward.

When World War II came along, I closed up my business; volunteered for the Army Air Force, where I became a flying instructor; and later a flight engineer on a B-29 bomber. During the war, I married my college girl friend, Elinor Healy in a wonderful marriage that has now lasted 68 years. In that war, I saw the joy and satisfaction of working together as a team, just as I had seen in High School, when I was a 120 pound end on the varsity football team.

Elinor Healy and I were married on August 29, 1943

Fishing in Florida. 1944

I saw that same spirit of cooperation and we can and we must attitude in our nation in the period following the war, as we all worked together CHARGING FORWARD after winning the war to build a nation that was the envy of the world. From the war until the early 70s, (the period Robert Reich, Secretary of Labor under President Clinton, called the period of Great Prosperity) our top income tax rate was about double what it is today. Corporations contributed about 30% of the nation's tax revenue, compared to the 9% they contribute today under our loophole ridden corporate taxes.

Many of my friends who returned from the war attended college, paid for by the GI Bill. For others the tuition at public universities averaged only about 4 percent of median family income.

**Elinor and I standing before one of the training planes
in which I taught young cadets to fly. 1944**

**I am standing on the far left. The other young men
are the rest of my B-29 flight crew. 1945**

After World War ll I returned to Iowa where I again opened up my fishing tackle factory that had been closed during the war. We continued to charge forward, concentrating on new and better products recognizing that REVENUE MATTERS and Berkley and Company continued to grow.

We began a family shortly after I returned from World War 2.
The three Bedell children, Joanne 1; Tom 3; and Ken 5. 1953.

It was my great honor, while still a Republican, to be recognized as the First National Small Business person of the year in 1964 by President Lyndon Johnson in a Rose Garden ceremony.

I receive the National Small Businessman of the Year award from President Lyndon Johnson in the Rose Garden of the White House with my family present. Ken is barely visible just to the left of the President. 1964

We arrive home in our own family plane after receiving
the Small Businessman of the Year award. 1964

Post card put out in the local area in about 1970,
when Berkley and Company had over 1,000 employees.

I obtained patents, which helped my company, but I saw how our legal and patent system adversely affects small business. It costs so much to defend your own patents, or to prove someone else's patents invalid that most small businesses cannot afford the court costs no matter how fraudulent a competitor's patent may be. For example, it cost my little company about $1 million to prove that a DuPont patent was invalid, a price too high for most small businesses to afford.

Just as significant is the fact that big business can afford to hire lawyers to defend themselves in court and lobbyists to get special treatment from government. Small businesses generally cannot do either. Small business provides most of the innovation and job growth of our nation, but we have policies that put it at a great disadvantage in competing with big business.

I was recognized as one of only two sitting members of Congress that had obtained patents. About 1982

I became more and more concerned over what I saw happening in our nation. On my 50th birthday I went to the County Court House and changed my registration from that of a Republican to that of a Democrat - whereupon my mother declared that she thought she would have to move out of town rather than suffer the embarrassment of living with a Democratic son in the same town, which had almost no acknowledged Democrats. I had never been active but I decided I wanted to try to do something about my concerns. I was particularly upset over our war in Vietnam. I decided to run for the U.S. Congress. I had a poll taken. The pollster said, "Don't run. You do not have a chance."

So, just as I toured the nation selling fishing leaders I did not know how to make, I charged forward. I ran. I lost.

But I surprised everyone by getting 49 percent of the vote, and two years later I was elected to the United States Congress as a

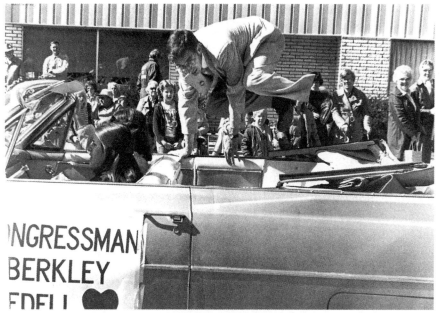

**In parades, I learned how to jump in and out of a convertible.
I would jump out, shake hands with some of the crowd and jump back in
while the convertible kept going down the parade route.
The crowd loved it. 1975-1987**

Democrat serving an overwhelmingly Republican district in Northwest Iowa.

I arrived in Congress in 1975 while our nation was still in the period of Great Prosperity. We still worked together, Republican and Democrat as a team, building a better nation. We cooperated for the

Speaker Tip O'Neill presents Reverend Ken Bedell with a certificate for giving the opening prayer to the House of Representatives. I am standing next to the speaker with House Majority Leader Jim Wright on my right. Next to Ken is Robert Bauman, Ken's Congressman, and Jim Ford, House Chaplain. About 1979

good of the nation. We recognized that REVENUE MATTERS. And we charged forward with a TOGETHER WE CAN attitude.

I could not believe my ears as I sat on the steps of the Capitol with other members of Congress just a few feet from the new President, Ronald Reagan, as he gave his inaugural address and proclaimed, "Government is the Problem."

Government has many problems. It is inefficient. It tends to be wasteful. Sometimes it over regulates and sometimes it under regulates. It can become consumed with partisan bickering. But with all its warts, it is the only institution that can prevent the powerful from exploiting the masses. It can cause a nation to charge forward and build a nation in which everyone cooperates and works together to share in the benefits of the nation's progress. Or it can cut back, cut taxes, and let the rich and powerful exploit the masses.

So now we had a President that did not believe in government and was going to let the rich and powerful take advantage of their power without a government to protect and help the people.

I was there when the nation caught tax cut fever. It started with Reagan's proposed major tax cuts, directed primarily toward the

Tom, Elinor and me with President Jimmy Carter at the White House picnic in 1978.

wealthy. But the Democrats did not oppose it. They joined in the game. Both sides tried to outbid the other by trying to propose the largest tax cuts. The Republicans won. I voted against the Reagan tax cuts, just as I would have done with the Democratic proposals.

I had learned in my business career that REVENUE MATTERS, and neither a business, or a government can do what needs to be done without sufficient REVENUE.

Many of my constituents were livid. "How could anyone vote against cutting people's taxes when it was promised that doing so would balance the budget?" I believe it was the best vote I cast in my 12 years in Congress. Those tax cuts started us down that slippery slope from Great Prosperity to Great In-

I present President Carter with a Berkley fly rod shortly prior to the end of Carter's four year term. 1980

equality, which has become more and more obvious as the wealthy 10 percent of our people own more and more of the wealth of our nation, and control both Congress and much of the media with their political contributions and ownership of Corporate America.

When he was leaving office in the late 50's, President Dwight Eisenhower warned of the increasing and dangerous influence of a military industrial complex - but we failed to listen. We proceeded to build a bigger and bigger military machine. Military might and reduction of taxes for the rich seemingly were more important than the kind of society we would have.

Wars inevitably followed as we flexed our military muscles. We went to Vietnam on the other side of the world. When we lost we

I address the Democratic National Convention on behalf of Small Business. 1984

should have learned some lessons about the limits of our powerful military machine and using it to try to impose our will on the world.

We failed to learn!

There were many unusual - even bizarre - aspects of the twin towers and Pentagon attacks by terrorists on September 11, 2001, but the roots of the killing of nearly 3,000 victims were hatred of America.

The terrorists came from bases in Afghanistan so we did what was natural for us; we invaded Afghanistan. The Afghanistan action is stretching on endlessly and like Vietnam, we do not seem to be close to victory.

We have failed to recognize that fighting and killing neither makes friends, nor builds a peaceful world. As with empire building nations throughout history, more of the world's people dislike us, and few want to follow our leadership.

Since the end of World War ll other nations have watched what has happened in our powerful nation. Their leaders have seen that by working together with a TOGETHER WE CAN attitude after World War ll we built a wonderful place to live. They also noticed what happened when we somehow let the rich and powerful take control of the government, diminishing the well being of ordinary citizens.

Progressive nations were instituting universal health care, taxing individuals based upon their ability to pay, and instituting shorter weekly hours of work. They rejected spending so much of their national wealth on the military. And they avoided the tremendous inequality of wealth that was building in the U.S.

In a democratic nation, people can choose what type of government and society they want. We can have Great Prosperity or Great Inequality. WE CANNOT HAVE BOTH.

At this time it appears that our federal government, particularly the Tea Party influenced Republicans choose inequality instead of prosperity as they cut taxes to the wealthy, and try to cut programs for the people.

So, as I come to the twilight years of my life, I hope that the message of this book will start to cause the people of our nation to see that it is time for us to again start to work together as we did in the middle of the last century and when I was first elected to Congress in 1975.

It is time for we voters to say to the politicians, "Put the lives of the people ahead of the wealth of a few, and to restore the great prosperity that we had when we taxed people and corporations according to their ability to pay and used that money to improve the lives of the people.

I outline in the book many of the things I think we are doing wrong as a nation, including:

1. A political system in which the wealthy and Corporate America control with their political contributions who is in Congress and how they will vote.

2. Failure to recognize the threat of a nuclear holocaust and the unwillingness to take a leadership role in leading the world to a planet free of nuclear weapons.

3. The pollution of our planet through the burning of fossil fuels which makes us more and more dependent upon imported oil and may make our planet unable to continue to support human life.

4. The failure of our government to recognize that REVENUE MATTERS and to tax those of us with the ability to pay and Corporate America to get the revenue needed to charge forward and return to the Great Prosperity of the past.

5. A partisan Supreme Court that, like today's Republican Party, represents the rich and powerful and corporate America rather than interpreting the laws of the land in a non-partisan manner.

Sometimes while I write I yearn for those days of my boyhood when we did not have large homes and multiple automobiles. We washed our dishes and clothes by hand. There was no television or computers. As a youth our recreation was playing hide and go seek, or riding our bicycles out to the swimming beach. In the winter we played outside in the snow, not inside watching television - and none of my buddies were obese. Most everyone was relatively poor by today's standards, but we worked together with what we had and life was good.

As we face the problems of unemployment, lack of universal health care, global pollution and a host of other problems, it is my hope that we may again see that we need to work together as we did in World War ll to save both the planet and our species and bring back the Great Prosperity we had during those years. We need to take back the government from the wealthy 10 percent of the people and Corporate America. We need to replace the can't do attitude with a TOGETHER WE CAN attitude and charge forward to return to the Great Prosperity of the past.

This book is an attempt by one human being with 90 years of experience to try to motivate the 90 percent of the common people to rise up and take back our government, so that we may move back from the current period of Great Inequality to the period of Great Prosperity I was able to experience in my earlier years. When politicians try to tell us what we can't do we need to shout back, "TOGETHER WE CAN and we will turn our nation around."

Chapter 2

GOVERNANCE

TOGETHER WE CAN turn the government back to the people.

Government action will be necessary if we are to make the changes necessary for a more equitable society with equal opportunity for all and compassion and concern for each other. Government action will also be necessary if we are to take the steps needed to preserve our planet; our survival may well depend on it.

Our forefathers had just fought a bloody Revolutionary War with Great Britain and its autocratic king when faced with the challenge of writing a Constitution and establishing a government for the new nation.

They wanted to be sure they established a government by and for the people. They wanted to be sure leaders and in particular the head of state, did not have too much power. So they provided for a President to be elected by the people, and a system of checks and balances with a system of three governmental branches. The Congressional branch enacted laws, the President applied them, and the Judiciary interpreted them.

This system with its three branches worked quite well for a long time. It served as an example for the rest of the world. As the nation and world progressed the Constitution was amended from time to time but our forefathers provided safeguards so that it could not be amended easily or without due consideration.

Although we had to make changes to broaden the franchise - enabling women to vote, providing for direct election of Senators by the voters, and mandating that everyone of age be able to vote - for a long time we truly had government of, by and for the people.

In recent years things have changed.

In 1972 when I first ran for the U.S. House of Representatives from a rural Northwest Iowa district, my campaign cost about $88,000--$25,000 of it out of my own pocket. I only had to raise $53,000.

Even back then, contributed money had an impact; I still remember some of my larger contributors in that first election. But back just those few years ago, money in politics was nothing compared to what it has become.

I had several advantages compared to most political candidates. I owned a successful business and had the money needed to finance my own campaign if necessary. After first being elected I was rarely seriously challenged and won every succeeding election with about 60 percent of the vote. And although I liked serving in Congress, I was not in love with the position or the power. If I lost, I had other things to do. But that is not the situation for most politicians--they must have the money for their next campaign.

In later campaigns my spending increased but, nonetheless, what I spent pales when compared to the average of over $1 million a House member now spends, and $7 million for a U.S. Senator.

I had a jolt, though, when I retired from Congress in 1986. I supported one of my staff members, Clayton Hodgson, in his bid to assume my seat. An agricultural political action committee pledged $2,000 to his campaign. When I voted in the agricultural committee against a bill the group supported, the PAC cancelled its pledge. If the money had been intended for my re-election I wouldn't have cared. But it bothered me that my vote had hurt my friend, who needed the money in his campaign.[1] It made me think about how I would have felt if I really needed that money for my campaign, as do most members of Congress.

As I saw with the cancelled pledge from the agricultural interest, political contributions influence most every vote of every member of Congress.

My wife and I spend our winters in Naples, Florida, where there is a large population of wealthy homeowners. To build a beautiful Philharmonic Hall they raised a lot of money from those wealthy

---

[1] He eventually lost to Fred Grandy, R-Iowa.

homeowners. Concerts and programs are conducted with the prices sufficiently high that the same wealthy individuals make up most of the audience. Few young workers and their families can afford to attend. Some seats are even labeled with the names of the individual or couple that made a significant contribution. Hardly anyone, rich or poor, objects to the "Phil". It is simply accepted that those who pay the bill should receive the benefits and programs should reflect the wishes of those who contribute. So it is with the federal government.

Follow the money: THOSE WHO MAKE THE CONTRIBUTIONS GET THE BENEFITS!

The problem is clear. Most members of Congress like the job and believe they are doing a good job. They believe that to get the money needed for their next election they have to keep their campaign contributors happy by voting as demanded by those contributors and their lobbyists.

Practically all of those campaign contributions come from the top 10 percent of our population and Corporate America, and that is whom the government serves, without regard for the middle class and 90 percent of the American people.

Clearly the wealthy and special interest groups have the money to give and the incentive to give it. When money is so important to political survival, contributors that give the most speak the loudest. For an industry to contribute $10,000 and get legislation that saves the industry $1,000,000 is a pretty good investment. It has properly been called *legalized bribery.*

Lobbyists' bad reputation is well deserved but they do serve a worthwhile purpose. As a member of Congress, it was impossible for me to know everything about every issue that came before me. By presenting their views, lobbyists help to properly inform all members.

The problem comes not from their information, but from their bags of money. Lobbyists bundle contributions from members or employees of the industry or company or interest group that the lobbyists represents. It sends a powerful message that if the politician wants that money for his or her next election he or she had better vote as the lobbyist wishes.[2]

Examples of how this works are too many to count, but one of the worst is the pharmaceutical industry's influence over Congress. From 1990 through October of 2002, the industry contributed about $125 million to Congressional and Presidential candidates, including money from individual PACs. That includes more than $18 million in the 2004 campaign alone, as reported by the nonpartisan Center for Responsible Politics. The pharmaceutical industry spends more on lobbying than any other manufacturing industry - and it pays off.

The United States is the only developed nation that does not in some way regulate drug prices. Not only do we not regulate drug prices, our federal government in a law passed by Congresspersons that receive large political contributions from the pharmaceutical industry, prohibits the federal agency that administers Medicare and Medicaid from trying to negotiate lower prices on pharmaceutical drugs! They can negotiate for lower prices in everything else they buy - from their pencils to their office computers - but not pharmaceutical drugs!

The second problem is that legislators spend a large part of their time on the telephone raising political contributions, instead of conducting their business.

In an effort to remedy this situation four former Senators-Bill Bradley and Bob Kerry, Democrats, and Warren Rudman and Alan Simpson, Republicans — are leading an organization called Americans for Campaign Reform to promote public funding of Congressional elections.

There are bills in both the U.S. Senate and House of Representatives calling for public funding of House and Senate campaigns. Arizona and Maine both have enacted public funding laws, which have worked very well. Unfortunately, the Republican appointees on the Supreme Court have struck down a provision that enabled "clean" candidates to get matching money if they were outspent by "non-

---

[2] And a recent ruling by the U.S. Supreme Court that corporations may now contribute with few limitations to political campaigns has compounded the problem. If we thought we had a problem before we had better watch what happens with this bad decision!

clean" opponents. However, this Supreme Court decision does not affect the bills in Congress, as none of them have such a provision.

Public financed elections have brought more responsive government for citizens in Maine, Arizona and other states. As Joe Bartholomew, a Maine legislator said, "The goal is to bring back the kind of democracy we learned about in grade school; campaigning on issues and qualifications rather than the money you can raise to buy TV ads."

These states have shown us that we do not need to continue with a government run primarily for those who furnish the money for political campaigns.

I believe that the most important change we can make in how our government functions is to pass public funding of Congressional elections, and take the influence of money out of our legislative process.

The same problem exists with presidential campaigns. An effort has been made to provide public funding for presidential campaigns but candidates have found that they can raise more money from donations than from the public funding schemes. This law needs to be changed.

There is another issue that has to do with the two-party system that has evolved in our federal and most state governments. In Congress the majority party elects the body's officers and determines the rules of operation. It is very important, especially now, to be the majority party.

When I was in Congress in the 1970s and 1980s the Democrats were in the majority, and it was accepted that in the next election the Democrats would continue to be in the majority. Since there was no fight as to who would be in the majority, it was in the interest of both Republicans and Democrats to work together in the best interests of the nation.

We did work together; some of my best friends were Republicans. Although the Democratic majority would try to convince the Democrats to vote according to the Democratic position, in my 12 years in Congress I never once felt that I had to vote according to the party position on any bill. I voted for what I thought was best for the nation, not always along party lines.

Then after I retired things changed. The Republican Party became more popular and the Democratic Party less so. It became a toss-up as to which party would be in the majority and run the Congress. Since it was of great advantage to be in the majority, members were pressured to vote according to what was perceived to be best for the party, rather than what was best for the nation.

Another problem has to do with the election of our president and vice president. When our well-meaning forefathers set up the provision for an electoral college to elect the presidential ticket, they messed things up by making the process more complicated than it needed to be. As everyone knows, the winner in each state receives a certain number of electoral votes and in most cases, the candidate with the most votes wins all of that state's electoral votes. This policy apparently originated when our country was founded in order to give adequate power to the less populated rural areas. Few people give much thought to the problem the Electoral College now causes.

The crux of the problem is that the percentage of Republicans and Democrats varies greatly from state to state. In some states such as Texas and Louisiana the Republicans outnumber the Democrats by such a margin that it is taken for granted that the Republican presidential candidate will safely carry that state. In others such as New York and California, it is taken for granted that the Democrat will win.

Then there are other states such as Florida and Ohio, where the electoral votes are up for grabs. It is known, for example, that in the 2000 election Al Gore received the most total votes, but because it was determined that George W. Bush won Florida, Bush was declared the winner with the most electoral votes.

In 2004, if John Kerry had won Ohio, he would have been declared the winner, even though Bush received the most votes nationally.

The problem is not just who wins and who loses. The problem is that the votes of those people in the safe states do not really count, whereas the votes of those people in the "battleground" states determine who will win.

If you live in Louisiana or New York there is not much incentive in your voting for President, as it is accepted that Louisiana will go for the Republican candidate and New York will go for the Democrat.

The system is so skewed that Matthew Dowd, a top campaign strategist for President George W. Bush admitted that they only polled in 18 states for the two years leading up to the 2004 election. The opinions and concerns of Americans in 32 states were not of concern to the Bush campaign team. It is no wonder that the Bush administration was so slow to respond to Hurricane Katrina. They had never learned how to get there. They had not made a single campaign visit to Louisiana during the fall of 2004, in contrast to 61 visits to Florida and 48 visits to Ohio.

It is a disgrace that over 30 percent of eligible voters do not vote in our country. But who can blame them in states where they know that their vote will not count? Looking at voters under 30, turnout was nearly 20 percent lower in safe states than in the 10 highest battleground states. It is apparent that nearly half of potential young voters in safe states decided there was no point in voting. It is certainly possible that we will never convince many of them to ever take part in American democracy.

At one time there was a real interest in solving this problem by both Republicans and Democrats alike. Presidents Johnson, Nixon, Ford and Carter all called for a national vote for President under the principle of one person one vote (the method that rules every election in this country except for President). In 1960 the House of Representatives overwhelmingly supported legislation calling for a one-person one vote national election for President. Such divergent groups as the AFL-CIO and the Chamber of Commerce backed it.

It is time to close the Electoral College and get back to true democracy with every vote being equal regardless of the state of your residence.

Let us also take a quick look at an alternative form of government. In many nations the majority party chooses the head of government. Citizens know whom to credit if things go well and whom to blame if they do not.

In the United States it is possible to have a Congressional majority of one party and a president of a different party.

It might be too much to suggest that we might switch to a completely different system of government, but it would be easy to change a small amount and elect members of Congress for four-year terms coinciding with the election of the President. This would offset the usual weakening of the Presidency due to normal losses in Congress in mid-term elections.

Another problem I want to put on the record is government regulations.

As we have seen failure to properly regulate the financial industry was a disaster. We need to properly regulate industry not to pollute. Without government regulations we would have a terrible mess - and we surely could not solve the planetary pollution problem.

But regulations needed to maintain a successful society, and regulations that unnecessarily interfere in the lives of the people are quite different.

For the government to tell me that I cannot have access to comparatively safe medical treatments being administered all over the world and to tell my farmer friend that he cannot sell his organic produce to those who want to buy it because he is not big enough to have a six foot fence around his farm to prevent a deer from entering his farm is, I believe, going overboard.

When I was a boy my grandfather had a few acres of land on which there was a lengthy grape vine. I picked and sold grapes to the local grocery store for 50 cents per bushel. Today I could not do that.

It is perfectly proper for the government to require that the public be informed that foreign medical treatments have not been FDA tested, or that the grapes are local produce, but a properly informed public should be able to make its own choices when such choices do not in any way harm society.

It is quite another thing when unregulated banks can bring about a financial meltdown with their gambling practices because of inadequate regulation-or when giant livestock feed lots are permitted to pollute the land.

Over and under regulation by governmental agencies has always been a problem. Now with the influence of corporate money in politics it has gained monstrous proportions as government regulators, like politicians, listen to the giant pharmaceutical companies and the major agricultural corporations.

So we find ourselves in a situation in which unregulated humans will surely pollute our planetary home to threaten our very existence without strong governmental regulations. And with a government filled with bureaucrats who love to unnecessarily regulate people's lives, causing the public to object to government regulations at a time when strong governmental regulations are imperative in some areas.

The challenge required if we are to address global pollution and other problems is to differentiate between those regulations that are necessary, and those that needlessly impinge upon the lives of the people.

A final big problem in our governance is caused by a thing called the filibuster. It is an almost sacred part of Senate rules and allows a 40 percent minority to block actions of the majority. It is hard enough to get a majority of Senators to vote to take strong steps, needed now more than ever; it is almost impossible if consent by a super majority is required as is now the case. We must insist on elimination of the filibuster in the Senate - if the folks now there will not do it themselves, we must elect people who will!

We have serious problems in our nation and the world but we also have the financial means to properly address these problems. To do so we must have a strong federal government that is not controlled by the campaign contributions of the rich and powerful.

TOGETHER WE CAN make our electoral system serve the people by removing the power of money with public financing of political campaigns; eliminating the electoral college; making sure regulations are based on common sense; and eliminating the filibuster.

Chapter 3

JOBS AND THE ECONOMY

*TOGETHER WE CAN put our people back to work
eliminating our planetary pollution, rebuilding our infrastructure
and bringing back the Great Prosperity of the past.*

I started my fishing tackle manufacturing business with one employee - me. When I turned it over to a new President, and went off to Congress we employed over 1,000 people. After going from one to one thousand, I think I know something about what it takes to increase jobs.

Creating jobs has nothing to do with cutting taxes to small business! As is pointed out elsewhere in this book, in the early years of my business career taxes were much higher than they are today, but that did not in any way hinder my growth or my ability to increase employment. I never ever made a business decision based upon tax considerations.

The main thing any business needs if it is to grow and increase employment is potential customers with the money to buy the products or services of the business. Today with the middle and bottom 60 percent of the people owning only 1 percent of the nation's wealth there is inadequate wealth in the masses to generate sufficient economic activity to provide the jobs needed to return to the Great Prosperity of the past.

A billionaire can only eat so much, and wear so many clothes. There is no comparison between what one family with a billion dollars of wealth can spend to energize the economy and what 10,000 families each worth $100,000 can do.

The jobs problem is easy to solve. All we have to do is to tax the wealthy and corporate America sufficiently to get the money needed to put our people back to work rebuilding our infrastructure; providing health care for all; providing for adequate retirement of our elders; making higher education available for all; and ending the pollution of our planetary home. As in the past, the tax revenues generated by people working will help solve our deficit problem — and the people working will spend money to provide jobs for others.

In a society, small business is the major job creator. I believe that is because small business tends to care about its employees; encourage creativity; and be close to its customers. Any successful small business recognizes that REVENUE MATTERS.

Each year as my company grew, the government was our partner. It furnished us the roads we needed to transport our fishing tackle to the dealers that sold our products. It furnished us the fire protection for our factory. It furnished the fishermen and women clean rivers and lakes in which they could use our products. It protected our factory and our employees from any thieves that would rob us.

It also did something vitally important to our growth, our revenue, and our increase in jobs! Particularly in the early years of our growth, it furnished us with a sufficiently large population with enough wealth that they could afford to purchase our products.

When it was formed our nation consisted mostly of farmers and farm families. It took a substantial percentage of our population to raise the food needed to feed all the people.

When I was a boy a significant number of my school buddies were from farms, where a 100-acre farm was considered normal. Today 1,000-acre farms are commonplace and many of the farmers in the area of my own home not only farm but also have other jobs in town. Tractors have replaced horses and mules; machines now pick the corn that was previously picked by hand. Meat and dairy products are now produced in factory farms with huge confined livestock operations. We have revolutionized farming so that only a small number of farmers are required to produce our food and fiber.

When I went to Congress in 1975 my fishing tackle manufacturing plant employed 1,000 people and had sales of about $20 million per year. Today that same business employs a similar number of people, but its sales are more than 10 times as much. It is amazing to walk through the factory and see machine after machine doing the jobs that we formerly did by hand.

In manufacturing as well as farming, machines replace more and more workers and fewer are needed to take care of our needs. This should be a blessing. We should be able to work fewer hours and provide a better living for all. But without government involvement corporations will increase workers' hours, reduce the pay of workers and increase the wealth of executives and stockholders.

Purchasing by the people fuels the economy but there is a vicious cycle when jobs are scarce. Unemployment reduces the purchasing of the people. Less purchasing reduces demand for goods and more unemployment. More unemployment further reduces the purchasing. It is a vicious cycle.

There are answers but they do not always come from the U.S. In 1982 labor unions in Holland agreed to limit higher pay in exchange for fewer hours of work. Within 10 years, the proportion of Dutch people working part-time increased from 19 percent to 27 percent while the average workweek fell from 30 hours to 27 hours. Unemployment dropped from 10 percent to 5 percent.

Germany and Austria have enacted laws that let employers avoid layoffs by scaling back workers' hours and pay. For example, 10 percent less pay for 10 percent fewer hours worked, with the government subsidizing the difference in pay.

U.S. workers historically have worked longer hours than those in other industrial countries. Our workers put in an average of 320 more hours per year (two months worth) than in France and Germany. If we were to adopt Germany's model it would theoretically provide additional employment for nearly 17 percent of our workforce and eliminate our unemployment problem.

One thing seems obvious in the United States.

Capitalism is in trouble in our country. Too many of our citizens are out of work. The wealthiest ten percent of our citizens are getting richer and richer, while the rest are falling further and further behind. Something is going to have to change.

Change is not going to happen in a country without the action of the federal government.

Today the best way to address the massive pollution and infrastructure problems we face is to use our creative industrial base to do the work and furnish the jobs - and tax ourselves, particularly the wealthy to provide the needed funds.

We clearly do not need everyone working 40 hours per week to take care of our basic needs. However, if we are to survive as a species, we urgently need to transform our current energy industry from polluting fossil fuels to non-polluting energy technology. Replacing our gasoline burning automotive fleet, converting our coal fired electrical plants, and doing all the other things necessary to save the planet requires two things - money and labor. The money is available by properly taxing the wealth of the wealthy and Corporate America. If it is used to put the unemployed to work the jobs crisis will be solved.

If there ever was an opportunity to make lemonade from a lemon, this is it.

TOGETHER WE CAN tax ourselves sufficiently to put our people to work rebuilding our nation and ending our pollution of the planet.

Chapter 4

SOCIAL SECURITY

TOGETHER WE CAN apply the Social Security tax equally to all, low and high income earners.

Social Security has been called the crown jewel of President Franklin Roosevelt's New Deal.

When it was enacted in 1935 the poverty rate of the elderly dropped by 50 percent.

But today because of our budget deficit some are calling on us to cut back on Social Security such as increasing the age at which one may qualify and retire. George W. Bush even tried to privatize Social Security, which as shown with the recent meltdown of the stock market, would have been a disaster.

Changing one of the most successful social programs of all time borders on insanity!

First of all, contrary to some claims, Social Security is not in financial trouble. The Social Security trust fund as this is written has a $2.8 trillion surplus that is expected to grow to $3.3 trillion by 2020. The Congressional Budget Office projects that Social Security can pay all of its scheduled benefits out of its own tax revenue stream for the next 25 years with no changes whatsoever.[3] Thus we have 25 years to fix future issues by, for example, properly taxing the wealthy, while continuing to provide benefits to society through a program that has stood the test of time since the middle of the last century.

---

[3] There is more of a problem with Medicare and Medicaid but it is caused by problems with our medical system, not our retirement program.

Secondly people need jobs. We need to have programs that encourage people to retire earlier so that there can be jobs for younger workers.

Medicare is in future financial trouble, but that should be addressed by reforming our health care system as recommended in a future chapter.

Today as people are losing their homes and other assets which they depended upon to help with their retirement, Social Security becomes more and more important to more and more retirees. However, the amounts paid through the system are frequently insufficient to provide for the type of retirement life they have been dreaming of as their wages stagnate and the wealthy take in more and more of the national income.

Both employers and workers fund Social Security through payroll taxes. But for some crazy reason instead of using a progressive system to increase the percentage high-income earners pay we do just the opposite.

We pay Social Security taxes on the first $106,800 of our income, which means that a janitor making $20,000 per year and his employer pay the full 12.5 percent while a banker making $500,000 and his employer pay less than 3 percent. The super rich do even better and of course hedge fund operators, some of whom who make a billion dollars per year, count their income as capital gains and pay no Social Security taxes at all.

In, 2010, 54,000,000 Americans were paying about $702 billion in annual social security taxes. Eliminating the $106,800 cap would, according to the Congressional Research Service, yield an additional estimated $129 billion, which would increase the income of the Social Security system by nearly 20 percent. That is to say that if we were to eliminate the cap so that the rich paid at the same rate as the workers, we could eliminate the so called funding problems for the social security system.

Social Security in America pays only 33 percent to 40 percent of a worker's pre-retirement earnings. In most of Europe that figures is 70 percent to 75 percent. Instead of talking about cutting back on Social

Security, we should be talking about finding ways to increase Social Security payments, particularly to those at the bottom of the income ladder.

By doing so we would not only help the retired elderly to live better lives, we would help the economy because their increased spending would help provide more jobs for our unemployed.

TOGETHER WE CAN eliminate the cap in the Social Security collection system so that high income workers pay the same Social Security tax rate as middle and low income persons.

Chapter 5

THE TAXPAYER
PROTECTION PLEDGE

A disaster for our nation.

This may be one of the shortest chapters in this book, but it is one of the most important. Every voter should be aware of what is in this chapter before they vote! The Taxpayer Protection Pledge makes the U.S. Congress unable to function in terms of addressing the problems that require Revenue — which is almost every function of government.

Not many people are aware of the influence of an organization called Americans for Tax Reform, or of their Taxpayer Protection Pledge — and the legislators who have signed it. This organization opposes all tax increases as a matter of principle, regardless of the situation. Their influence has expanded as corporations and the wealthy have become more powerful in controlling governmental policy with their political contributions.

IT IS VITAL THAT THE VOTERS BE AWARE OF THIS PLEDGE, WHICH GUARANTEES THAT OUR CONGRESS WILL NOT ADDRESS OUR NATION'S PROBLEMS.

According to Americans for Tax Reform as of October 2011, 235 Congressional House Members (A majority of the House) and 41 Senators have signed a pledge not to raise any taxes, no matter what the situation. All but two in the House and 1 in the Senate are Republicans. Here is what the pledge is reported to say:

"I (name here) pledge to the taxpayers of the (x) district of the state of (x) and to the American people that I will: 1. Oppose any and all efforts to increase the marginal income tax rates for individuals and/or businesses, and 2. Oppose any net reductions or elimination of deductions and credits, unless matched dollar for dollar by further reducing tax rates."

This pledge commits those who signed such a pledge to refuse to increase taxes on corporations and those of us who can afford to pay higher taxes no matter what the circumstances. It prohibits Congress from closing any of the tax loopholes that enable General Electric to pay no federal income taxes.

To have over half the members of the House and 41 Senators sign such a pledge may please major corporations, and some of the wealthy, but it makes our federal government essentially non-functional and is a disaster for the people of our nation. As long as such a large number of members of Congress have signed such a pledge there is no hope of our nation charging forward to address our problems until we throw out those pledge signers, including the three Democrats, and replace them with legislators that represent the people, not just their wealthy and corporate campaign contributors.

WORDS CANNOT PROPERLY EXPRESS WHAT A DISASTER THIS IS FOR OUR NATION AND FOR THE PEOPLE.!

Today, as is pointed out elsewhere in this book, billionaire Warren Buffet pays taxes at a lower rate than his secretary; many of the wealthy are even asking that their taxes be raised; high income individuals pay Social Security taxes at a lower rate than minimum wage earners; deductions enable some major corporations pay no income taxes; our taxes as a percent of GNP are lower than most all of the major industrial nations; our current taxes as a percent of GNP are the lowest in half a century; nearly 10% of our people cannot find a job; we are firing teachers, police, fire fighters, and other government employees because of a lack of revenue; our infrastructure is crumbling; and we need to switch over from fossil fuels to not-polluting energy. We cannot do the things that will take us out of our current economic meltdown without the revenue needed to do so — And those pledge signers have pledged not to do what has to be done to solve our unemployment problem, correct our deficit and bring back the Great Prosperity we once had.

At this time we face a major decision as to what type of nation we want to be. We can be a cut-back nation or a charge forward nation. As a democracy, it is up to us. If we want to end our partisan bickering and work together as we did in the past, it is imperative that we remove those who have signed this taxpayer's protection pledge and replace them with legislators that recognize that REVENUE MATTERS and return us to government of, by, and for the people.

The 13 Republican members who are reported to have NOT signed the pledge as of October 2011 are these:

Six Republican House member non-signers:
Richard Hanna, NY, Bob Woodall, GA., Rodd Russell Platts, PA., Bob Wittman, VA., Frank Wolf, VA,. And Kevin Yoder, KS.

Seven Republican Senate non-signers:
Richard Lugar, IN., Charles Grassley IA., Olympia Snowe, ME, Susan Collins, ME., Thad Cochran, MS., John Barraso, WY., and John Hoeven, ND.

Three Democrats are reported to have signed:
House members, Robert Andrews, NJ, Ben Chandler, KY, and Senator Ben Nelson, NE.

There is only one way to get back to a functional government that taxes corporations and the wealthy sufficiently to put our people back to work and to address our many problems. IN THE NEXT ELECTION VOTERS MUST KICK OUT THE THREE DEMOCRATS AND ALL THE REPUBLICANS THAT HAVE SIGNED THIS PLEDGE! Thank God we have a democracy where the people have a voice in who is in our government.

People have a choice. They can listen to the slick ads paid for by the political contributions of corporations and the wealthy and send back politicians that will sign pledges not to properly tax those who can afford it. Or we can get up off our fanny and go vote to return us to a nation that charges forward, puts our people back to work addressing our problems without signing pledges that make our government non-functional.

IT IS UP TO US!

Chapter 6

AMERICAN LEGISLATIVE
EXCHANGE COUNCIL

TOGETHER WE CAN elect legislators that represent we the people.

If you are not wealthy, or a legislator, you probably are not aware of the many right wing organizations partly funded by Charles and David Koch, two of the wealthiest industrialists in our nation. They include the Cato Institute, a libertarian think tank; Americans for Prosperity Foundation; Freedom Works, which was largely responsible for the creation of the Tea Party; and the National Taxpayers Union.

Eclipsing all of those right wing organizations is the American Legislative Exchange Council (ALEC) that in recent years has reported about $6.5 million in annual revenues. ALEC's members include corporations, trade associations, think tanks and nearly one third (about 2,000) of the nation's state legislators (virtually all Republicans). ALEC has two sections,"Public Sector" members (legislators) and "Private Sector" members (Corporations and special interest groups).

According to the group's promotional material, ALEC's mission is to "advance the Jeffersonian principles of free markets, limited government, federalism, and individual liberty, through a non-partisan public-private partnership of America's state legislators, members of the private sector, the federal government and the general public."

ALEC currently claims more than 250 corporations and special interest groups as private sector members. The organization refuses to make a complete list of these private members available to the public, but some of the known members include Exxon Mobil, the Corrections Corporation of America (Operates prisons for profit), AT&T, Pfizer Pharmaceuticals, Time Warner Cable, Comcast, Verizon,

Wal-Mart, Phillip Morris International and Koch Industries, along with a host of right-wing think tanks and foundations.

ALEC has nine task forces: 1.Public Safety and Elections; 2.Civil Justice; 3.Education; 4.Energy; environment and agriculture; 5.Commerce; Insurance and Economic Development; 6.Telecommunications and Information Technology; 7.Health and Human Services; 8.Tax and Fiscal Policy and 9.International Relations. Each task force is composed of both legislators and private sector members. Each task force generates model legislation that is then passed on to member legislators for introduction in their home assemblies.

So we have legislators meeting with Pfizer and Philip Morris to fashion legislation that is then passed on to nearly one third of the nation's state legislative members (about 2,000) for introduction in their state legislatures. If the provided figures are correct, (nearly one third of all legislators --nearly all Republicans) it would mean that over half of all Republican legislators are members of ALEC along with many of the giants of industry.

ALEC claims to have drafted 826 pieces of legislation that were introduced nationwide in 2009, with 115 of them passed into law. That means that an average of 2 pieces of legislation were enacted per state, that were formulated with the help of people representing firms like Exxon Mobile, AT&T, Pfizer, Wal-Mart, Philip Morris, and Koch Industries.

The Wisconsin effort to attack unions, and cut taxes to business and the wealthy has been front page news. What is not generally realized is that ALEC legislation, similar to that in Wisconsin has been introduced in Arizona, California, Illinois, Iowa, Indiana, Kansas, Maine, Maryland, Michigan, Minnesota, Missouri, North Carolina, New Hampshire, New Jersey, New Mexico, Ohio, Oklahoma, Rhode Island, Tennessee, Texas, Utah and Vermont.

This is not government of, by, and for the people!

As I point out in this book, I believe the wealthy and Corporate America are running our federal government, and our Supreme Court. It was a shock to me to learn that they are apparently also running our state legislatures using the Republican members of ALEC.

We have Republican appointed Supreme Court Justices ruling that corporations can give political contributions. We have Republican legislators meeting with corporations to fashion legislation favorable to those corporations. This is not the Republican party of previous times, and the Republicans with whom I served in the U.S. Congress.

TOGETHER WE CAN take back our state and federal governments and turn America around to again have a government of, by, and for the PEOPLE.

Chapter 7

THE TEA PARTY AND THE CONTRACT FOR THE AMERICAN DREAM

TOGETHER WE CAN follow the example of the Tea Party,
and take back the government for the people.

David and Charles Koch are two of the nation's wealthiest business persons. They did not become that wealthy by making stupid decisions.

One of their best investments, ever, was the funding of the start of a new movement called the Tea Party. The Kochs, or someone advising them, recognized that a significant proportion of our population is upset with what they see happening in our nation and would like to have an opportunity to demonstrate their frustration.

So the Koch brothers helped to fund the beginning of this movement of frustrated individuals, called The Tea Party.

It is not surprising that many of the non-wealthy 90 percent of the people would be upset and frustrated. With the top 10 percent of our people and Corporate America owning more and more of the total wealth of our nation, while everyone else sees their incomes stagnate or declining it is understandable that people are upset. Thank God they are! The last thing we need in America is a complacent population.

As those Tea Party members looked at whom to blame, there was only one obvious culprit - the federal government. So the simple answer was, to cut back the federal government by reducing government spending - and reducing taxes.

By enrolling a large number of frustrated voters, the Tea Party had a significant influence in the most recent election and it now is a major influence in our government, particularly the Republican Party. Their power is intoxicating.

As is so frequently true, their simple answer may appear to be the best answer for the Koch brothers, but it is exactly the wrong answer for 90 percent of the people.

The best thing for the Koch brothers, and the rest of the wealthy and Corporate America may appear to be to continue to cut taxes to the rich, and cut services for the people - exactly what the Tea Party advocates. The worst thing for the other 90 percent is to continue to cut services to the people, and continue to cut taxes for the rich.

The Tea Party has shown us what can be done when the people get sufficiently upset. It is up to the rest of the nation to learn from their example, and take back the government so that it serves the 90 percent of the people that combined have less than 20% of the nation's financial wealth and are struggling.

Those of us who care about our country, need to follow the example of the Tea Party. We need to organize and make our voices heard.

Since I started to write this book, a new organization has sprung up to challenge the Tea Party proposals. It is called the Contract for the American Dream. It takes its name from a speech by Reverend Martin Luther King, Jr. during the 1963 march on Washington, when he said, "I have a dream. It is a dream deeply rooted in the American Dream." The movement already boasts over a quarter of a million signers, and is growing every day. Here is the movement's statement:

> *"We the American people promise to defend and advance a simple ideal: liberty and justice for all. Americans who are willing to work hard and play by the rules should be able to find a decent job, get a good home in a strong community, retire with dignity, and give their kids a better life. Every one of us - rich, poor, or in-between, regardless of skin color or birthplace,*

no matter their sexual orientation or gender - has the right to life, liberty, and the pursuit of happiness. That is our covenant, our compact, our contract with one another. It is a promise we can fulfill - but only by working together.

Today, the American Dream is under threat. Our veterans are coming home to few jobs and little hope on the home front. Our young people are graduating off a cliff, burdened by heavy debt, into the worst job market in half a century. The big banks that American tax-payers bailed out won't cut homeowners a break. Our firefighters, nurses, cops, and teachers - America's everyday heroes - are being thrown out onto the street. We believe:

AMERICA IS NOT BROKE. America is rich - still the wealthiest nation ever. But too many at the top are grabbing the gains. No person or corporation should be allowed to take from America while giving little or nothing back. The super-rich who got tax breaks and bailouts should now pay full taxes - and help create jobs here not overseas. Those who do well in America should do well by America.

AMERICANS NEED JOBS, NOT CUTS. Many of our best workers are sitting idle while the work of rebuilding America goes undone. Together, we must rebuild our country, reinvest in our people and jump start the industries of the future. Millions of jobless Americans would love the opportunity to become working, tax-paying members of their communities again. We have a job crisis, not a deficit crisis.

To produce this Contract for the American dream, 131,203 Americans came together online and in their communities. We wrote and rated 25,904 ideas. Together, we identified the 10 most critical steps to get our economy back on track and restore the American Dream.

10 CRITICAL STEPS TO GET OUR ECONOMY BACK ON TRACK

1. *Invest in America's infrastructure.*

2. *Create 21st. Century Energy Jobs.*

3. *Invest in public education.*

4. *Offer Medicare for all.*

5. *Make Work Pay.*

6. *Secure Social Security.*

7. *Return to fairer tax rates.*

8. *End the wars and invest at home.*

9. *Tax Wall Street speculation.*

10. *Strengthen Democracy."*

This is the type of movement by the people that I had hoped would develop. I have signed up.

We now have an alternative to the Tea Party. It is an opportunity we needed. Instead of cutting back as is proposed by the Tea Party, we now have an organization that proposes that we charge forward and build the nation that we have always dreamed of.

When the Tea Party and their Republican friends tell us we cannot tax the wealthy and corporate America to return to the Great Prosperity of the past our answer must be a loud and clear. TOGETHER WE CAN charge forward with a Contract for the American Dream!

Chapter 8

THE SUPREME COURT

TOGETHER WE CAN bring back a Non-partisan Supreme Court

One of the big shocks of my life was when the Supreme Court interfered with the Florida election recount to give George Bush the victory over Al Gore.

My latest shock came when the Supreme Court ruled in THE CITIZEN UNITED CASE that corporations could make political contributions.

Our forefathers who wrote the Constitution providing for "government of, by, and for the PEOPLE" would be aghast.

It is bad enough to have Republican legislators supporting corporate America with corporate tax cuts and fewer environmental regulations. It is quite another thing to increase the influence of corporations by letting them use their profits to purchase the votes of legislators.

Both my parents, and my only brother were attorneys, and the judicial system in Iowa has always been non-partisan. When I was in politics, federal judges could not participate in any of my political events.

Cannon 5 of the Code of Conduct for United States Judges states: "A judge should not ... make speeches for a political organization ... or attend or purchase a ticket to a dinner or other event sponsored by a political organization or candidate ... A judge should not engage in any other political activity."

The Code further states: "The term "political organization" refers to a political party, a group affiliated with a political party or candidate for public office, or an entity whose principal purpose is to advocate for or against political candidates or parties in connection with elections for public office."

I had always assumed that the Supreme Court Justices would have to abide by the same regulations as the federal judges in my former Congressional district. Unfortunately that is not necessarily the case.

The framers of the Code of Conduct for United States Judges states that the Code "applies to United States circuit judges, district judges, Court of International Trade judges, Court of Federal Claims judges, bankruptcy judges, and magistrate judges." It failed to mention Supreme Court Justices.

You would think that judges on the highest court of the land would have to abide by the same rules that apply to other federal judges. In fact Supreme Court justices, Kennedy and Breyer both testified before the House Appropriations Financial Services Subcommittee on April 1, 2011 that the Court has agreed internally to be bound by the Code.

David and Charles Koch are billionaire industrialists who are credited, among other things, of financing the start up of the Tea Party movement. The Koch brothers have organized political gatherings of wealthy individuals to try to influence them to support government policies that cut back on governmental policies that help the people and cut back on taxes and regulations on the wealthy and Corporate America. It is reported that the January 2011 Koch event in Rancho Mirage, California raised $49 million to be used in the 2012 election cycle.

The invitation to that event by Charles Koch stated "PAST MEETINGS HAVE FEATURED SUCH NOTABLE LEADERS AS SUPREME COURT JUSTICES ANTONIO SCALIA AND CLARENCE THOMAS ..."

So, we have Antonio Scalia, Clarence Thomas, and the three other Republican appointed justices voting in the 5 to 4 CITIZENS UNITED VS. FEDERAL ELECTIONS COMMISSION case to change the law so that corporations can act as if they are persons, and make political contributions from corporate funds.

As is pointed out elsewhere in this book, we already have the wealthy with their political contributions practically owning both the Republican Party, and the government, as well as owning most all of the wealth of the nation. To throw corporate wealth into the system is like pouring gasoline on a fire.

If anyone has felt as I do that the influence of money in politics is bad for the people of the Nation. Hang onto your hat!

Since some of the Republican appointed Supreme Court justices do not believe they have to abide by the rules restricting political activity that apply to most all other federal judges, those of us who believe in "Government of, by, and for the PEOPLE", better make sure that we do not elect a Republican President that can stack the Court with another Republican judge that could make the Court even more partisan.

TOGETHER WE CAN - elect a government that will reverse the current 5 to 4 Republican appointed majority on the Supreme Court, and change the code of conduct so that the Court will again become the non-partisan Court it once was--and reverse the Citizens United decision that pretended that corporations are citizens.

Chapter 9

THE BUDGET AND TAXES

TOGETHER WE CAN raise the tax revenue to put our people back to work, rebuild America and return to the Great Prosperity we once had.

During my term in Congress, I was one of the few former business persons in the United States Congress. In business I learned one basic lesson. Whether it is a business, your family finances, or government there is one basic law it is REVENUE MATTERS.

Today too many in our federal government led by the Tea Party Republicans are ignoring that basic law.

I was in Congress when our government caught "tax cut fever". When Ronald Reagan said that individuals could spend their money more wisely than the government, many persons agreed.

But that is not the issue; instead questions like these should be asked:

- What do you think is more important, the education of our youth or a larger home?

- Which is needed more, health care for all or a bigger automobile?

- What must we have to survive, a livable planet or more stuff?'

We need to ask ourselves, "What do we have to do to build the kind of nation and world we want?" And even more important, "What do we have to do to survive as a species?"

It has been said that those who ignore history do so at their peril and we are doing exactly that today

In the Roaring '20's the rich became richer and richer. The wealthiest one percent of the population received 23.9 percent of the nation's total income in 1928. The rich did not productively spend that vast income, instead speculating and making risky investments with their money. In 1929 there was a massive market crash that led to a severe depression and the Great Depression followed.

The government was forced to come up with solutions and stepped in with New Deal programs such as the Works Progress Administration, the Social Security Act, United States Housing Authority and Agricultural Adjustment Act.

World War II and the GI Bill helped bring about a more equal society and by the 1970's the richest one percent was down from 23.9% to about 9% of our total national income. We prospered--it has correctly been called the period of Great Prosperity.

The massive tax cuts primarily for the wealthy under Presidents Reagan, George H.W. Bush, and President George W. Bush, together with our wars in Iraq and Afghanistan caused our deficits to boom and our financial inequality to explode.

By 2007 the richest one percent in this country were back where they were in 1928 with over 23 percent of the nation's total income. In 2008 we nearly repeated the Great Depression.

We need to look at what happened from 1994 until 2001 during the administration of President Clinton. In his first year in office, President Clinton pushed through a tax increase that fell almost exclusively on the upper income taxpayers. Republicans incorrectly claimed it was the "largest tax increase in history".

Here is what happened:

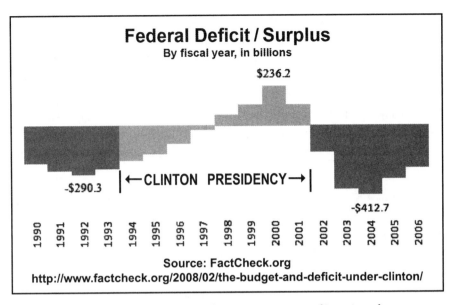

Federal Deficit / Surplus
By fiscal year, in billions

$236.2

←CLINTON PRESIDENCY→

-$290.3

-$412.7

1990 1991 1992 1993 1994 1995 1996 1997 1998 1999 2000 2001 2002 2003 2004 2005 2006

Source: FactCheck.org
http://www.factcheck.org/2008/02/the-budget-and-deficit-under-clinton/

Here are my proposals for financing a new direction for our nation and the planet. Their implementation and costs will not significantly affect ordinary people and even if they do, returning to the Great Prosperity and saving the planet will certainly be worth it.[4]

Because the U.S. military budget is now nearly equal to what the rest of the world's countries spend *combined*, we should reduce our military expenditures of $607 billion by 50 percent - 10 percent per year for 5 years. In a lot of ways, all our giant military does is cause us to be disliked and get us into trouble around the world.

As we should have learned with the invention of nuclear arms, the more powerful weapons we develop, the more other nations will acquire such weapons and the threat to us will increase, instead of decreasing.

If we cannot defend ourselves by spending more than twice that of our closest rivals, something is wrong. Of course, we cannot do this overnight but we need to start the process. A 50% reduction once completed would save us more than $300 billion introduced at a rate of $60 billion per year.

---

[4] Keep these figures in mind; our total annual federal expenditure, including defense, social security and everything else was $3.8 trillion in 2010, income was $2.4 trillion, and the deficit $1.4 trillion. It is projected to decease as we wind down the war in Afghanistan and do not need to continue to rescue the financial sector.

Under President Eisenhower, the top income tax rate was 91 percent. Even with the loopholes, it was roughly double our current top rate of 35 percent. In 2010 our income taxes brought in about one trillion dollars. We need to get back to those tax rates we had when I came to Congress when we had Great Prosperity. According to the Congressional Research Service, this would at least double the current income tax revenue of one trillion dollars, which together with the cut in military spending would practically wipe out our current deficit.

Today we tax increases in property value--capital gains--at a lower rate than earned income. It makes no sense that wealthy persons should pay lower taxes on the increase in value of their property than workers do on their wages-- this lower tax messes up our whole economy. It causes investors to gamble on investments that qualify for the low capital gains tax, rather than regular interest income. The federal government lets hedge fund managers who gamble for the wealthy and make themselves billions of dollars per year count their income as capital gains; while wage earners pay regular income taxes. We should index capital gains to cover the loss of value through inflation, and then tax it as regular income.

With inflation, a dollar invested last year is today probably worth less than it was one year ago. For example, if I invest $100 today and sell that investment for $110 after a period of time during which inflation has decreased the value of my money by five percent, I have really profited only $5. I should only have to pay taxes on the actual $5 profit, but that $5 should be counted and taxed at the regular income tax rate. Tables could easily be furnished that show the amount of inflation from the time of purchase to the time of sale. The Congressional Research Service was unable to give me an estimate of the amount of increased revenue such a change would bring about, but it would be substantial. I estimate it to be about $300 billion per year.

Here's another-- a textbook look at so-called "death" taxes:

- The IRS collects the *estate tax* on U.S. citizens and residents. It is levied on a deceased person's estate as a whole and paid out of the estate's funds. There is a $5 million exemption for 2011 before an estate will be taxed.

- Some states impose additional estate taxes or *inheritance taxes* on beneficiaries who receive property from the deceased. This varies from state to state.

Lottery winners must pay state and federal income tax on winnings. Persons who inherit money pay no federal inheritance tax and in most states, no state inheritance tax. We should eliminate estate taxes, and tax inherited money the same as lottery earnings - regular income. It makes no sense that income received from a rich uncle's estate should be treated any differently than lottery winnings. If taxed at the Eisenhower rates, it is estimated by the Congressional Research Service that such a tax would raise about $177 billion per year.

Across the nation, Indian tribes have built gambling casinos. The tribes have recognized how people love to gamble. Many states have instituted lotteries and legalized and taxed Indian casinos to cash in on this tendency.

Nobel-winning economist James Tobin proposed in 1972 a tax that would place a penalty on short-term speculation in speculative financial instruments. It is known as the Tobin tax and is the kind of measure that should be adopted to discourage the money market gambling that almost brought about a second depression. Annual world derivatives trades were reported in 2008 to be $1.14 quadrillion ($1,140 trillion - the figure is probably low because over-the-counter trades are unreported).

Over half of these transactions take place in the Unites States. A tax of .1 percent (1/1000) on the United States trades would discourage gambling. The Congressional Research Service estimates that if the $1,140 trillion figure is correct such a tax would generate about $570 billion per year. This proposal is just for derivatives; it does not include stocks, bonds, and other financial trades. Of course, such a tax would discourage some of the wealthy who gamble on these instruments to cut back on their trading - -but that in itself would make a meltdown less likely in the future.[5]

In 2008 the U.S. Government Accountability Office reported that 83 of the 100 largest publicly traded corporations, including AT&T, Chevron, IBM, General Electric, Boeing, Dow and AIG, have subsidiaries in other countries; they are offshore tax havens.

General Electric had an effective tax rate of minus 15.8 percent between 2006 and 2010. Citizens for Tax Justice estimates that corporate loopholes will cost the U.S. Treasury Department $365 billion in 2011.

As is pointed out in Chapter 4, wage earners only pay Social Security taxes on the first $106,800 of their earnings. Removing that earnings cap, so that people with high incomes would pay at the same rate as low income persons would bring in an estimated additional $129 billion per year as estimated by the Congressional Research Service.

In 2010 Dieter Lehmkuhl delivered to German Chancellor Angela Merkel a petition he and 43 other rich Germans had signed. It urged a five percent wealth tax for two years to fund programs that would aid German economic and social recovery. The petition said, "The path out of the crisis must be paved with massive investment in ecology, education and social justice." The Congressional Research Service has estimated that such a tax in the United States, applied only to the wealthiest one percent of the population, would raise about $122 billion per year.

If we are going to survive as a species, we have to have a planet that can sustain human life. Unless we address the problem of global pollution, including the carbon dioxide we pour into the atmosphere, our very survival as a species is threatened. A tax on polluting carbon would make alternative energy sources more competitive and help to save our species. Such a carbon tax would be applied at the source of the problem, such as coal-fired electrical generating plants and petroleum refineries. The tax could start at a modest $50 per ton

---

[5] If Europe did not institute a similar tax, much of the trading in derivatives might go to Europe. However, the European Union has already indicated an interest in such a tax to help finance efforts to address global warming.

of carbon dioxide emitted and could be increased as necessary to give alternative energy sources a competitive advantage over such polluters. Such a tax would not be paid directly by the public; it has been estimated that it would raise the price of gasoline by about 40 cents per gallon and electric rates by about 3 cents per kilowatt hour, but it would make alternative energy sources, such as solar and wind energy, even more competitive with gas, oil and coal. I am advised that a $50 per ton tax would raise about $300 billion per year.

So, as is said, "show me the money" - here it is:

ITEM	NEW REVENUE PER YEAR
Military spending cut	$60,000,000,000
Tax rates adjustments	$1,000,000,000,000
Capital gains reform	$300,000,000,000
Inheritance taxes	$177,000,000,000
Financial gambling taxes	$570,000,000,000
Offshore tax havens	$365,000,000,000
Removing the S. S. cap	$129,000,000.000
Five percent wealth tax	$122,000,000,000
$50 per ton carbon tax	$300,000,000,000
Total new revenue per year	**$3,023,000,000,000**

(Over 3 trillion dollars)

This is much more than the total current federal deficit! It is much more than we need--and it is just additional REVENUE. Of course, I am not proposing that we institute all of these changes. It is just to show you the potential that exists.

Except for second and last item, these items would have little or no direct impact on 90 percent of the people.

Whenever taxes are increased (which does not happen very often) the wealthy scream and the public joins in. But keep in mind during the Clinton Presidency, taxes were raised not once, but twice. The economy boomed, and we had a government budget surplus.

Our forefathers felt that taxes should be based on ability to pay and we need to reinstate that position. When we do there will be funds available that can be used for the work of rebuilding a planetary home on which we can survive and thrive—and bring back the Great Prosperity we had when we charged forward as a team and created the revenue needed to build a better society for all.

TOGETHER WE CAN charge forward, recognizing that revenue matters and taxing those who can afford it to bring back the Great Prosperity of the past.

Chapter 10

WARREN BUFFETT AND THE PATRIOTIC MILLIONAIRES

Warren Buffett is one of our nation's wealthiest individuals. Here is an op-ed piece he wrote which appeared in the 08/15/2011 New York Times newspaper:

"Our leaders have asked for "shared sacrifice." But when they did the asking, they spared me. I checked with my mega-rich friends to learn what pain they were expecting. They, too, were left untouched.

While the poor and middle class fight for us in Afghanistan, and while most Americans struggle to make ends meet, we mega-rich continue to get our extraordinary tax breaks. Some of us are investment managers who earn billions from our daily labors but are allowed to classify our income as "carried interest," thereby getting a bargain 15 percent tax rate. Others own stock index futures for 10 minutes and have 60 percent of their gain taxed at 15 percent, as if they'd been long term investors.

These and other blessings are showered upon us by legislators in Washington who feel compelled to protect us, much as if we were spotted owls or some other endangered species. It's nice to have friends in high places.

Last year my federal tax bill - the income tax I paid, as well as payroll taxes paid by me and on my behalf - was $6,938,744. That sounds like a lot of money. But what I paid was only 17.4 percent of my taxable income - and that's actually a lower percentage than was paid by any *of the other 20 people in our office. Their tax burdens ranged from 33 percent to 41 percent and averaged 36 percent.*

If you make money with money, as some of my super-rich friends do, your percentage may be a bit lower than mine. But if you earn money from a job, your percentage will surely exceed mine - most likely by a lot.

To understand why, you need to examine the sources of government revenue. Last year 80 percent of these revenues came from personal income taxes and payroll taxes. The mega-rich pay income taxes at a rate of 15 percent on most of their earnings but pay practically nothing in payroll taxes. It's a different story for the middle class: typically, they fall into the 15 percent and 25 percent income tax brackets, and then are hit with heavy payroll taxes to boot.

Back in the 1980s and 1990s, tax rates for the rich were far higher, and my percentage rate was in the middle of the pack. According to a theory I sometimes hear, I should have thrown a fit and refused to invest because of the elevated tax rates on capital gains and dividends.

I didn't refuse, nor did others. I have worked with investors for 60 years and I have yet to see anyone - not even when capital gains rates were 39.9 percent in 1976-77 - shy away from a sensible investment because of the tax rate on the potential gain. People invest to make money, and potential taxes have never scared them off. And to those who argue that higher rates hurt job creation, I would note that a net of nearly 40 million jobs were added between 1980 and 2,000. You know what's happened since then: lower tax rates and far lower job creation.

Since 1992, the I.R.S. has compiled data from the returns of the 400 Americans reporting the largest income. In

1992, the top 400 had aggregate taxable income of $16.9 billion and paid federal taxes of 29.2 percent on that sum. In 2008, the aggregate income of the highest 400 had soared to $90.9 billion - a staggering $227.4 million average - but the rate paid had fallen to 21.5 percent.

The taxes I refer to here include only federal income tax, but you can be sure that any payroll tax for the 400 was inconsequential compared to income. In fact 88 of the 400 in 2008 reported no wages at all, though every one of them reported capital gains. Some of my brethren may shun work but they all like to invest. (I can relate to that.)

I know well many of the mega-rich and, by and large, they are very decent people. They love America and appreciate the opportunity this country has given them. Many have joined the Giving Pledge, promising to give most of their wealth to philanthropy. Most wouldn't mind being told to pay more in taxes as well, particularly when so many of their fellow citizens are truly suffering.

Twelve members of Congress will soon take on the crucial job of rearranging our country's finances. They've been instructed to devise a plan that reduces the 10 year deficit by at least $1.5 trillion. It's vital, however that they achieve far more than that. Americans are rapidly losing faith in the ability of Congress to deal with our country's fiscal problems. Only action that is immediate, real and very substantial will prevent that doubt from morphing into hopelessness. That feeling can create its own reality.

Job one is for the 12 to pare down some future promises that even a rich America can't fulfill. Big money must be saved here. The 12 should then turn to the issue of revenues. I would leave rates for 99.7 percent of taxpayers unchanged and continue the 2 percentage-point reduction in employee contribution to the payroll tax. This cut helps the poor and middle class, who need every break they can get.

But for those making more than $1 million - there were 236,883 such households in 2009 - I would raise rates immediately on taxable income in excess of $1 million, including, of course, dividends and capital gains. And for those who make $10 million or more - there were 8,274 in 2009 - I would suggest an additional increase in rate.

My friends and I have been coddled long enough by a billionaire-friendly Congress. It's time for our government to get serious about our shared sacrifice."

Warren E. Buffett is chairman and
chief executive of Berkshire Hathaway.

In a similar effort, over 100 wealthy persons, calling themselves, "Patriotic Millionaires, sent the following letter to President Barack Obama, Harry Reid, and John Boehner.

Dear Mr. President, Hon. Harry Reid, and Hon. John Boehner;

We are writing to urge you to put our country ahead of politics.

For the fiscal health of our nation and the well-being of our fellow citizens, we ask that you increase taxes on incomes of over $1,000,000.

We make this request as loyal citizens who now or in the past earned an income of $1,000,000 per year or more.

Our country faces a choice - we can pay our debts and build for the future, or we can shirk our financial responsibilities and cripple our nation's potential.

Our country has been good to us. It provided a foundation through which we could succeed. Now, we want to do our part to keep that foundation strong so that others can succeed as we have.

Please do the right thing for our country. Raise our taxes.

Thank you.

Patriotic Millionaires,
574 Broadway, Suite 1012, 10th Floor
New York, NY 10012
Reprinted by permission from The Patriotic Millionaires

The Patriotic Millionaires had some correspondence with Senator Orrin Hatch, a top Republican on the Senate Finance Committee, in which Senator Hatch argued against raising taxes on the wealthy. Senator Hatch told them that they could voluntarily contribute if they thought their taxes were too low. Here is their reply:

Dear Senator Hatch,

Thank you for your letter of April 20. With all due respect, you appear to be laboring under a number of misapprehensions. On behalf of the "so called" (your word) Patriotic Millionaires we would like to take this opportunity to set the record straight.

First we are well aware that making voluntary contributions to reduce the deficit is an option that is open to us. That you seem to think reminding us of this is a constructive contribution to this serious debate indicates that you have missed the point. In our democracy, individual citizens do not get to pick and choose what government spending to pay for. You and your colleagues over the past decade have voted for vast outlays that many of us as individuals might not agree with. Nonetheless, we recognize our responsibility as citizens to pay for those expenditures, which were authorized by our elected representatives, and are therefore ultimately our collective responsibility. That is an intrinsic part of living in a democracy: you don't get to opt out.

But letting people opt out is precisely what you are suggesting with your proposal of paying down our debt with voluntary contributions. In World War II, when we faced great challenges as a nation, we didn't ask for voluntary contributions to pay for the war, or ask only those who supported the war to contribute. We had high taxes during the war, and high taxes to pay down the debt, afterward. Today we benefit from that fiscal discipline. But we are undoing those benefits to society by cutting taxes on the wealthy at the same time we face enormous expenses and are carrying enormous debt. We need all of the above to address this problem, just as we have done in the past.

During World War II, we even resorted to rationing to share the burden of war more equitably. Who is paying the burden of war today? Our less privileged, who fight and die in disproportionate numbers, and our future generations, who will bear the burden of the debt. We think that is shameful.

We are willing to step up to the plate with a willingness to sacrifice for the greater good but we are not willing to make that sacrifice in vain, which it surely would be if we *followed the course you suggest. You even point this out yourself in your letter when you note that "the Bureau of Public Debt recorded only $3.1 million in gifts in 2010." We have been more fortunate than most people, but we are a very small group. If there were even the remotest chance of making a noticeable dent in the problem by acting alone we would have done it already. But we are a few dozen people in a nation of over 300 million facing a debt measured in tens of trillions. To suggest that we try to tackle this problem by making individual contributions is, frankly insulting. It is like suggesting to someone expressing a desire to serve their county by bearing arms that they buy a rifle and plane ticket to Afghanistan. Some problems are too big to be solved except through collective effort and shared sacrifice, and this is one of them.*

Second you write: "this debt crisis is not caused because we tax too little. It is caused because our nation spends too much." This is quibbling over semantics. Deficits result when spending exceeds receipts. Whether that happens because spending is too high or receipts are too low is a matter of perspectives and priorities.

In 1977 when you first became a Senator, the U.S. National Debt was approximately $700 billion---that's with a B – or 36% of then GDP. At the end of 2008, before Barack Obama came to the White House, the National Debt ballooned to almost $10 trillion – that's with a T and about 70% of the 2008 GDP (OMB). While there are different opinions as to how this happened, the National debt did not creep up on us suddenly. The spending that led to such debt resulted from the collective actions of Senators and members of the House of Representative, including you.

It is true that government spending levels are at historic highs, but it is also true that tax rates (and hence receipts) are at historic lows in terms of percentage of GDP. It is a combination of these two factors that has taken us from surplus to near-catastrophic deficits in a mere decade...

The second historical point is that we have faced a crisis like this before. In the early 1990's we successfully addressed a similar crisis through a combination of tax increases and spending cuts. As a result, in 2000 we were not debating how to address a debt crisis, but rather how best to dispose of a budget surplus. It is also worth noting, as a matter of historical fact, that we reached this happy state of affairs through a bipartisan effort involving a Democratic President and a Republican Congress. This makes us fundamentally optimistic that the problem we face today is surmountable.

You close by expressing concern about raising taxes on us "during a vulnerable economic recovery." It is precisely because we do not want this problem solved solely on the backs of the most vulnerable that we have asked the President to call us to duty. To him and to you we say again: raise our taxes. We can take it.

Both letters reprinted by permission of the Patriotic Millionaires

If we will follow the advice of Warren Buffett and the Patriotic Millionaires, TOGETHER WE CAN do as we did during and after World War II, and again in the early 1990's by taxing the wealthy sufficiently to get the Revenue needed to bring back the Great Prosperity of the past.

Chapter 11

FINANCIAL INEQUALITY

*TOGETHER WE CAN reduce our current financial inequality
and bring back the Great Prosperity of the past.*

As long as there has been money and trade among humans, there has been financial inequality. Those with holdings could lend their money at interest and increase their wealth; others would be unable to accumulate enough to lend and get interest.

Sometimes inequality came from a person's birth. Kings, queens and emperors lived the life of royalty. But most people lived with hardship getting by on the largess of the rulers.

The New World changed this. Alexis de Tocqueville traveled throughout the United States in 1831 and recorded his impressions.

> *"Among the new objects that attracted my attention during my stay in the United States, none struck me with greater force than the equality of conditions. I easily perceived the enormous influence that this primary fact exercises on the working of the society."*

For a long time gains in total wealth were a blessing. Increased wealth in a country and its accompanying higher standard of living made it possible for wealthy societies to enjoy better education, better health and medical care, more mobility and more leisure.

It is not surprising that the economic success of a nation was judged by the amount of its gross national product with little or no consideration given to how that GNP was being used or how equitably it was distributed.

But once a nation becomes sufficiently prosperous to provide for the basic needs of its entire people, GNP becomes a poor measure of the well-being and happiness of its people.

In one of his greatest speeches, Robert Kennedy said, "GNP measures everything...except that which makes life worthwhile...it tells us everything about America except why we are proud to be Americans."

In the early part of the 20th century the rich were becoming richer and richer until one percent of the population was getting nearly 24 percent of the nation's income. The Great Depression followed.

New president Franklin Roosevelt took action. New Deal programs such as the Social Security Administration, Works Progress Administration, Public Works Administration, United States Housing Authority, and Fair Labor Standards Act became the law of the land. The income of the top one percent came down to between six percent and nine percent of the nation's total.

World War II followed and fortunately we saw even more clearly what humans can do if they decide to cooperate instead of to just compete.

After the war we were the envy of the world but a sequence of terrible tax decisions and some needless wars began to change that.

Under President Eisenhower in the 50s the top income tax rate was 91 percent and the percentage of the nation's income in the hands of the most well to do one percent remained modest. The change began with Nixon's presidency in the 70s when the top income tax rate was lowered to 70 percent. Under Reagan it was lowered further to 50 percent. And under George W. Bush it was lowered still further to 35 percent.

As long as the Smiths and their neighbors the Joneses had similar incomes and wealth there was no need for the Smiths to try to keep up with the Joneses in both income and consumption. Both families were content and happy and enjoyed each other's company.

Then Mr. Jones became CEO of a major corporation, whereupon the Joneses' income increased to twice that of the Smiths. The Joneses bought a bigger house and car and the Smiths borrowed all they could to try to keep up with the Joneses. But the Joneses found that it did not make them happier to have a bigger car and house. The Joneses in their new house no longer enjoyed the friendship of the Smiths. Even with their big mortgage, the Smiths could not keep up with the Joneses so Mrs. Smith found a job to try to help them keep up with the Joneses. She no longer had the time to help the family's children with their homework - she yearned for the good old days when they were happy with what they had and enjoyed the picnics and family evenings with the Jones family.

So it has happened across the country as increased inequality has led people to reduce their savings, increase their bank overdrafts and credit card debt, and arrange second mortgages to fund consumption to try to keep up with the Joneses.

Authors Richard Wilkinson and Kate Pickett[6] spent years researching the effect of inequality on societies. What they found should not surprise anyone - the greater the financial inequality in a society, the lower the society ranks in the things that are important in life. The information in the Wilkinson and Pickett book has helped me write much of this chapter.

The United States has the greatest financial inequality among all the industrial countries of the world. We have by far the largest prison population. The four nations with the least inequality in the world are Finland, Japan, Norway and Sweden. They also are the four nations with the smallest percentage of their people in prison. Japan has only 40 persons in prison per 100,000, less than eight percent of the rate in the United States, and Finland, Norway and Sweden are close behind Japan.

Within our country the pattern is the same. Louisiana, the state with the second highest amount of financial inequality, imprisons people at more than six times the rate of Minnesota, one of the states with the least inequality.

The United Nations Children's Fund rates international child well being by examining 40 different indicators. It is not surprising

---

[6] Their book is, The Spirit Level: Why More Equal Societies Almost Always Do Better.

that Finland, Norway and Sweden rate highest in terms of childhood well being. Nor is it surprising that the U.S falls among the four lowest countries in terms of childhood well being.

Foreign Aid is another measure of a nation's concern for others. Again, there is no surprise. Portugal, Norway and Sweden give the highest percentage of their national income for foreign aid; the United States the lowest.

It should also surprise no one that the United Nations World Drug Report shows Finland, Japan and Sweden are also low in illegal drug use. And, of course, the U.S. is one of the top four nations on the illegal drug use index.

In regard to health, looking at what happened during the two World Wars will teach us much. In the decades during which the wars took place, life expectancy increased between six and seven years for both men and women. In the decades before, between and after, life expectancy increased only between one and four years. Living standards declined during both wars but there was full employment, and income inequality declined. The resulting sense of cooperation, greater financial equality and social cohesion not only led to better health but crime rates also declined.

Teen pregnancies are highest in the nations with the highest income inequality. The United States has a teen-age birth rate more than 10 times higher than Japan.

Social mobility is the opportunity for a youngster to move up the financial ladder as compared to his or her parents. Social mobility increased in the United States until tax revisions kicked in with an accompanying explosion of financial inequity; a dramatic decrease in social mobility followed.

It is quite clear to me that growing financial inequality in our country increases health problems, health care costs, violence, prison populations and teenage pregnancies, and that it reduces social mobility, happiness and compassion.

There are a few examples that might make my fear of what is happening in America more understandable even if it sometimes seems appallingly incomprehensible. Knowing that one percent of the rich folks receive 24 percent of the total annual income, what about the super-rich?

The family of Wal-Mart founder Sam Walton has a combined fortune of about $90 billion; in 2005, Bill Gates was worth $46 billion and Warren Buffet $44 billion. By contrast, in the same year the total wealth of the bottom 40 percent of our population was estimated to be $95 billion. Consider this; the wealth of the Walton's, Gates' and Buffet was almost double that of 120 million persons. If our tax policies had resulted in the wealth of the three to be half what they are, the increased revenue would have been equal to the amount needed to double the wealth of the bottom 40 percent of our people—that bottom 40% of our people now have trouble paying their mortgages, getting health care, and sending their kids to college - and the Walton, Gates and Buffet families would not exactly have had to scrimp with a combined wealth of $90 billion.

As one can see, from the graph at the beginning of this book, ten percent of our people now have 82 % of the financial wealth of the nation (net worth minus net equity in owner-occupied housing). Even more shocking is that 20 percent of the people now own 93 percent of the wealth. That leaves only 7 percent of the total wealth of the nation to take care of all the lower and middle class. It is the purchasing power of the lower and middle class that creates a vibrant economy and provides the jobs of a society.

As long as almost all of the political contributions come from that top 20 percent and politicians do the bidding of that 20 percent to get the funds for their next campaign, we will continue to have a nation with a small number of wealthy plutocrats and the bulk of the population struggling to get by. If we want to get back to the Great Prosperity we had in the earlier years of my life, we have to take the money out of politics by passing public funding of Congressional campaigns, properly tax that 20 percent, and use the increased revenue to eliminate the deficit and improve the lives of the people.

The tremendous financial inequality shifts our attention from the pressing environmental and social problems and focuses our attention on jobs, security, and how to get the economy moving again. Putting an end to that inequality would enable us to build a society where we once again cooperate to build the Great Prosperity we once had.

The writers of my Christian Bible recognized the problem when they quoted Jesus in Matthew 19: 21-25.

> *"If you wish to be complete go and sell your possessions and give to the poor, and you shall have treasure in heaven, and come follow me." But when the young man heard this statement, he went away and grieved; for he was one who owned much property. And Jesus said to his disciples, "Truly I say to you, it is hard for a rich man to enter the kingdom of heaven." And again I say to you, "It is easier for a camel to go through the eye of a needle than for a rich man to enter the kingdom of God."*

And again in Matthew 6: 2

> *"You cannot serve both God and mammon (material wealth)."*

TOGETHER WE CAN recognize the magnitude of the financial inequality problem; take back the government by passing public funding of congressional campaigns; throw out the can't do, cut back TEA PARTY REPUBLICANS; and bring back the Great Prosperity of the past.

Chapter 12

THEODORE ROOSEVELT'S SPEECH

TOGETHER WE CAN learn from former
Republican President Theodore Roosevelt.

My friends, Chuck Collins and Sam Pizzigati, wrote the following article, which appeared in The Progressive Populist.

"Ex-Presidents almost always follow a small number of well-worn scripts. Some rush to cash in on their celebrity. Some do charitable good deeds. Some just lie low.

One century ago, on August 31, 1910, we had an ex-President who took the brash and bold leap that took him far beyond the narrowly circumscribed roles. On that day, in the Middle of America, a former President - Theodore Roosevelt - essentially called on his fellow citizens to smash the nation's rich down to democratic size.

We need, Roosevelt told a massive assembly of 30,000 listeners to 'destroy privilege.' Ruin for our democracy he warned, will be 'inevitable if our national life brings us nothing better than swollen fortunes for the few.'

Those listeners - in Osawatomie, Kansas - roared their approval. Back East apologists for grand fortune would be aghast. Editorial writers would label Roosevelt 'frankly socialistic,' even 'anarchistic.' A later historian, George Mowry, would call TR's talk, soon to be known as his 'New Nationalism' address, 'the most radical speech ever given by an ex-President.'

Time hasn't dimmed that radicalism. Indeed TR's speech speaks powerfully to us today, mainly because we confront, a hundred years after he spoke in Osawatomie, the same concentrated wealth and power the TR so feared.

As president between 1901 and early 1909, Roosevelt had taken on a plutocracy just as entrenched as ours today. He won some battles and ducked many others. But he left the White House feeling the nation, under his successor William Howard Taft, would be headed in the right direction.

But Taft disappointed Roosevelt and outraged the progressive wing of Roosevelt's Republican Party. TR saw a burning need to spell out a clearer vision for his nation's future, and he jumped at the invitation from Osawatomie to help dedicate the historic small city's John Brown Memorial Park.

The event quickly figured to be the biggest in Kansas political history. Roosevelt had just finished a triumphal global tour. He ranked, observers agreed, as the 'world's most popular citizen.'

Kansans would pull out all the stops to set the stage for a memorial speech. By the appointed day, Osawatomie had never looked better. Bands and dignitaries would be everywhere.

'We are ready for plutocrat and peasant', wrote one local editor. 'To honor the ground where John Brown made his decisive stand for freedom.'

Plutocrats never did show. But average Kansans did. They started coming the day before TR's scheduled appearance, in a driving rain, via foot, bicycles, motors, buggies, vans, and trains.

The rain fortunately, would stop before the mud became too deep. Roosevelt would have open skies when he stepped up onto his podium, a kitchen table, to begin his address. 'The surging throng,' says historian Robert La Forte, 'continually cheered,' for the next hour and a half.

Most Americans today would cheer too. Are you outraged by the BP oil disaster in the Gulf of Mexico? Our national resources, Roosevelt pronounced, 'must be used for the benefit of all our people, and not monopolized for the benefit of the few.'

'The Constitution guarantees protection to property and we must make that promise good,' Roosevelt noted. 'But it does not give the right of suffrage to any corporation.'

We must 'prohibit the use of corporate funds directly or indirectly for political purposes,' TR enunciated, and hold corporate officials 'personally responsible when any corporation breaks the law.'

Again and again, Roosevelt urged his listeners to demand state 'and especially national restraint upon unfair money-getting.' The absence of that restraint he noted 'has tended to create a small class of enormously wealthy and economically powerful men, whose chief object is to hold and increase their power.'

But TR didn't stop there. Restraining fortunes based on 'unfair money-getting' had to be only a first step. A fortune 'gained without doing damage to the community,' he added, deserves no praise. Americans needed to set a higher standard. We should permit fortunes 'to be gained only so long as the gaining represents benefit to the community.'

And even those fortunes, Roosevelt added, needed to be checked, because 'the really big fortune, the swollen for-

tune, by mere fact of its size acquires qualities that 'differentiate it in kind as well as in degree from what is possessed by men of relatively small means. Qualities that help ensure the political domination of money.'

To check the growth and limit the power of these fortunes, Roosevelt called for a progressive income tax and an 'inheritance tax on big fortunes properly safeguarded against evasion and increasing rapidly in amount with the sizes of the estate.'

Three years after TR's Osawatomie speech, we would have an income tax in the United States. Six years later after Osawatomie, we would have an estate tax. By the middle of the 20th century many of the reforms that Roosevelt demanded on that August day a century ago would be the law of the land.

By the mid century, the plutocracy that Roosevelt decried had essentially disappeared. The United States had become a middle class nation where average workers, as TR envisioned in 1910, had 'a wage more than sufficient to cover the bare cost of living, and hours of labor short enough to leave them time and energy to bear their share in the management of the community.'

Now that mid 20th century middle class has disappeared. We live amid plutocracy once again.

A hundred years ago, Theodore Roosevelt refused to accept these sorts of concentrations of enormous wealth. At Osawatomie, he helped inspire a generation-long struggle to break up these concentrations. That struggle succeeded.

Our struggle has only just begun. We can succeed too."

Reprinted by permission of "The Progressive Populist."

This article points out the situation we find ourselves in today.

Roosevelt had a great advantage over those of us who believe that a strong middle class and adequate income for the masses makes for a better society. Roosevelt lived before television, and the explosion of the cost of campaigning, which have enabled the wealthy to buy Congress, and to influence the media through their advertising payments and outright ownership of television and the media.

Today the wealthy can fund a Tea Party movement and a media blitz that confuses people into thinking the answer to our problems is to cut taxes to the rich and cut help to everyone else.

By the middle of the last century, as a result of actions taken after Roosevelt's speech, the income of the top two percent had dropped to approximately eight percent of the nation's total income. Automobile factory workers made nearly double what they do today and our society was the envy of the world. We need another leader like Teddy Roosevelt to help mobilize the other 90 percent.

TOGETHER WE CAN heed Roosevelt's message to bring back the Great Prosperity that existed during the middle of the last century.

Chapter 13

CAPITALISM AND CORPORATIONS

*TOGETHER WE CAN regulate and control Capitalism
and Corporations so that they serve the people, not just the wealthy.*

As the human species advanced on the planet, money was invented and *ownership* became more general.

Humans began to own land as well as chickens and hogs, houses and furniture, and finally cars, airplanes and ships. Many liked the system and some of them almost came to worship what they called capitalism. This was especially true in the United States where it became almost sinful to criticize capitalism.

But there are problems with capitalism.

In capitalist societies individuals, associations, corporations or governments own almost every material thing. Particularly with individuals the more one owns the better he or she lives and often the more they are admired.

Capitalism is a tremendous motivator; greedy humans tend to work hard to own as much as possible. Several years ago, while visiting China, I learned that its overall production of goods and services nearly doubled when workers benefited directly from their labor compared to when all shared its rewards equally under communism.

But capitalism has no conscience.

Throughout human history the tendency has been for the strong to exploit the weak. The best fighters even made slaves of those they conquered. Victorious conquerors lived lives of privilege and the weak were at their mercy.

Until the American Civil War, wealthy persons in parts of our nation had slaves while poor people scratched out a living. A person owning 100 slaves could produce nearly as much as 100 individuals. The wealth that could be accumulated went well beyond living expenses and the wealthy tended to accumulate more and more wealth.

Emancipation and the Industrial Revolution changed things. Machines became the slaves and the wealthy people who owned enough machines could also increase their wealth beyond belief.

Common ownership of the factories and machines that produced the wealth was an opportunity thought to be open to all when stock in companies was offered through a stock market. The theory was a good one, but most people working for wages had to use most of their earning to provide for themselves and their families---there was little or nothing left to invest in the stock market or any of the other investments available to the wealthy.

Those who had excess income, in some cases many times what was necessary for living expenses invested the surplus and became even wealthier. Ironically the world cheered at the supposed benefits of trickledown economics while the rich got richer and the poor became poorer.

Capitalism is a tremendous motivator...We need to completely retool our energy industry to make it non-polluting; we should take advantage of capitalism's motivation to accomplish it while at the same time providing jobs for our people

But the facts are clear---unrestrained capitalism results in greater and greater economic inequality; and increasing inequality has a deleterious effect on all classes in a society, not just the poor.

As our nation grew, money was needed to fund the factories and commercial enterprises. The world's largest stock exchange, the New York Stock Market, was established in 1792 to facilitate buying and selling the shares of corporations. Prices were determined by the performance of the corporations and the demand for their stock.

When the United States began to industrialize in the 19th century, buying stock in corporations became a popular way for people to share in the profits of the Industrial Revolution. It was a win-win process. Corporations were provided the money they needed to buy machinery and grow their businesses; ordinary people were given an investment opportunity that offered them the chance to receive money as the businesses grew and prospered as well as from the dividends paid by corporations to owners of their stock.

As corporations compete, they work to reduce costs to compete. I successfully started my business because my costs were lower than any of my competitors. To compete, corporations will do all they can to reduce their cost of labor. Two of the ways they can do that is either lowering wages, or moving work overseas to low wage countries. Either of these is devastating to nations that depend upon the income of the people to furnish the purchasing power to drive the economy. During the period of the Great Prosperity labor unions represented about one third of the workers. They were able to demand and get fair wages for the workers. Now our government and corporate political power has enabled corporations to break the power of labor unions, and corporations have held down the worker's wages, which has helped to create our economic downturn.

Corporations have brought us many improvements to our lives, including better washing machines and fishing tackle. But they also are responsible to a large degree for the tremendous financial inequality that exists in our nation.

Europe has avoided some of this problem. Labor unions are still strong in most of Europe. Europeans work shorter hours, and have more vacations. They can spend more time with their families. They have better benefits, and serve on company boards of directors as pointed out later in this chapter. We need to learn from what Europe has done to prevent the abuses of corporations.

Instead of limiting the power of corporations to adversely affect our economy, the Republican influenced Supreme Court has said that corporations can contribute to politicians to further their opportunity to adversely affect our economy and create even greater financial inequality.

I understand corporations. For a large part of my life I managed a corporation, Berkley Fishing Tackle Company, making fishing tackle. We were a family owned business and we cared about our employees. Our primary goal was, "to provide a better life for our employees and their families," as compared to the goal of most other corporations – "making money for their executives and stockholders".

I knew that when I had all the wealth I needed, profits could better be used to provide for a better life for our employees and their families than to simply make me richer.

I had learned from my participation in high school sports and my service in World War II that teamwork works and I tried to install a team spirit in our corporation, where we cared about our workers and their families.

It worked and we prospered.

In the period of Great Prosperity during the middle of the last century we had strong labor unions, government-mandated minimum wages, and a 40-hour week with time and a half for overtime. Executive pay was relatively modest. Worker's wages increased; inequality declined, and our society prospered.

Then things started to change. Government became pro-business, instead of pro-society. We cut back on government regulations; made it harder for unions to organize; let inflation reduce the minimum wages and lowered taxes on businesses and rich people. We did not realize what corporations would do in an unregulated business environment.

Weak labor unions and the absence of government regulations led to corporations reducing workers wages while at the same time increasing executive compensation and ultimately bringing on the period of what I call Great Inequality.

Today we have a minimum wage that is not sufficient. The federal minimum is $7.25 per hour. Based on working 40-hour weeks, 52 weeks per year this is an annual gross salary of $15,080. The yearly poverty rate for a family of four is $21,756. Surely the minimum wage should at least equal the poverty level! We cannot hope to decrease the number of Americans living in poverty until this happens.

Compared to our $15,080 annual minimum wage, the minimum wage in Britain is approx $22,597, or about 50% higher. Denmark, one of the economic stars of Europe does not have a legislated federal minimum wage. They do not need it. The labor unions, which are strong in that nation, negotiate a minimum wage, which is practically double that of Britain, and nearly 3 times ours--$44.252. Argentina's surpasses that of Britain. Belgium, Canada, France, Ireland and the Netherlands all have higher minimum wages than ours. As I have already pointed out, it is the income of the common people and middle class that drives the economy. We cannot build the nation I want to see by not paying people enough to keep them out of poverty. But if our lawmakers try to raise the minimum wage lobbyists for the U.S. Chamber of Commerce and its members scream that it will be another reason for our corporations to move more and more jobs overseas.

There are many ways to keep our jobs here. The way to do it, however, is not by paying our workers pauper's wages while some corporate executives make out like bandits, being compensated at levels well beyond any imaginable need.

Many worldwide duties are already in place. It is recognized that they protect local workers and industry and that they are legitimate and necessary. For example, if Mexico had enacted an adequate duty on corn imports to keep out heavily subsidized U.S. corn, Mexican farmers would still be able to make a meager living growing corn instead of crowding Mexican cities or trying to cross the border into the U. S.

Corporations are created to make money. If they can legally pollute the planet they will do it. If they can legally lower the pay of their workers they will do it. If they can avoid taxes they will do it. If they can control Congress with their political contributions they will do it.

I have a friend, John Limpittlaw, who is an Episcopal Priest. He spent a good share of his life in Corporate America. In middle age he decided he wanted to do something more personally rewarding and became a priest. Here is what he wrote me.

"When I left Warnaco and joined Macmillan in 1977 the salaries of the CEO's of the two companies - both in about the middle of the Fortune 500 - were $150,000

and $175,000 respectively. By 1990 the total compensa-
tion of Warnaco's CEO was $25 million; Macmillan's
CEO, who joined the company just eight years before,
walked away with a "golden parachute" of over $100
million.

Why the extraordinary rise in top management compensation over the last 25 years? Because of the use of
stock options and stock grants in executive compensation. Prior to 1980 (the period of the Great Prosperity),
few corporations used stock options as a method of compensation. As the stock market began its ascent in the
80s, following a decade in which stock prices had been
relatively flat, stock options began to be seen as a less
costly way of compensating executives. Cash compensation was a direct operating cost to the corporation while
stock options were not.

The effect of stock options, however, was not limited to
those who received them. An executive with a company
that included stock options might see his total compensation inflate dramatically. To compete for or retain
persons they considered to be top managers other companies would find it necessary to raise salaries of executives who had not received stock options as part of their
compensation package. This had a spiraling effect on executive compensation.

By 2000 the average compensation of Fortune 500 CEOs
had risen to $2.5 million - sixteen times what it was 25
years earlier (during the period of Great Prosperity).

There are two additional factors that contributed to the
rise in compensation. First, the outlandish salaries paid
in the 80s and 90s to Wall Street investment bankers.
And second, what I call the Chivas Regal effect - if we
are paying someone more than our competitors then he
must be better than the rest. This is not unlike the rise

in college tuition; that is, if a college charges less than Harvard, it must be inferior.

When I was a trainee in the 50s at Marine Midland Trust Company, the CEO earned $50,000 a year or about 14 times the salary of the lowest paid employee. That multiple for current United States CEOs is 289."

Reprinted by permission.

My friend accurately reports what has happened in America. Europe's inequality problem is not nearly as great as ours and we need to look at the reason. Part of it has to do with how corporations are run there.

After World War II, a group of prominent German economists proposed what they called a "social market economy," believing that the market should serve broader social goals. It was the conservative Christian Democrats, not the more liberal Social Democrats, who proposed this. The allied powers encouraged such thinking, because it decentralized German industrial power, which had been a major contributor to the German war machine.

So we punished a defeated Germany by encouraging democratic corporate capitalism that reduced the concentration of wealth and power and eliminated some of the most severe problems with strictly corporate capitalism.

Today Europe's democratic corporate capitalism has many qualities that outshine Wall Street corporate capitalism and without the extreme economic inequality in America.

German law provides that workers elect representatives to serve on the boards of directors (called supervisory boards). In Germany, the workers elect fully half the members of the boards of the largest corporations, such as BMW, Daimler, and Siemens.

This may seem like a small thing but it completely changes the corporate model from one that exists to benefit only the stockholders and executives to one that benefits the workers and society as well. Its effect upon society is enormous. Imagine what it would do to Wal-Mart if half its board of directors represented its employees.

German corporations give consideration to workers as well as executives and investors and the result is that the German people work fewer hours per year and experience less unemployment. The nation does not face the giant inequality that plagues America.

Much of Northern Europe has adopted corporate programs similar to Germany's. By giving workers a say, workers and management cooperate to keep the corporation competitive with benefit for the worker, stockholders and executives as well as all of society. Democracy in the workplace is just as important as democracy in government.

With corporate democracy, Europe, after being nearly destroyed by World War II, has become an industrial giant. Today Europe as a whole has the world's largest economy. It produces nearly a third of the world's gross domestic product. It has more Fortune 500 companies and its economy is larger than the economies of the United States and China combined. The World Economic Forum in 2008-09 ranked Denmark, Finland, Sweden, Holland, and Germany among the 10 most competitive economies in the world. All of them have some form of democratic corporate capitalism. They also rank high on most lists in regard to quality of life, health care and social benefits - lists on which the United States ranks near the bottom.

Europe does have a financial problem because of its common currency. I am not an expert on the financial problems of Greece, Italy and some of the other Southern European economies, but that does not detract from the successful economies of central and northern Europe.

I learned a long time ago that when someone else finds a better way of doing things, you should learn from them and adopt their methods. My fishing tackle manufacturing business would not have even been able to start if I had not found out how others were making fishing leaders.

TOGETHER WE CAN learn from what is happening in Germany and Northern Europe and replace our Wall Street Corporate Capitalism with a system of Democratic Corporate Capitalism to reverse the period of Great Inequality and move towards another period of Great Prosperity.

Chapter 14

WALL STREET AND THE MARKETS

TOGETHER WE CAN turn Wall Street and the markets into entities serving the nation, rather than gambling houses for the rich.

When I was in Congress I served on the House Agriculture Committee. We had jurisdiction over the commodities markets - Board of Trade and the U.S. Commodities Futures Trading Commission. I learned things that I had never considered as a businessperson.

The Hunt brothers were two wealthy Texans who tried to corner the silver market and nearly succeeded. We had them before our committee. I asked them, "Why would you want to do this when you already have more money than you can spend, and it would mess up our whole country?" They had no answer. It was an example of how unregulated humans can cause trouble in a capitalistic society.

The futures market for commodities was originally developed in order to help entities that needed to make sales or purchases in the future. A farmer could sell his crop on the futures market and be sure of the price at harvest; an airline could buy fuel on the futures market and know what their cost would be in the future. There was only one problem. In order for the farmer to sell his grain at a given price in the future, someone had to agree to buy it at that price. That person usually turned out to be a gambler who thought he could sell the farmer's grain for more than he had agreed to pay the farmer for it.

Since the boards of trade were run by humans who received commissions on their trades, they tried to do everything they could to increase the number of trades. They turned into giant gambling casinos with gamblers that had no grain to sell or fuel to buy making up the bulk of their traders. Gambling does nothing for the economy and I questioned at the time whether the benefits of the futures markets justified the negative effects of the gambling.

Corporations, communities and others also sold bonds to raise money on which interest was paid. In order to encourage investment in government facilities, such as schools and government buildings, the interest on many of these bonds was not subject to income taxes.

During the period of Great Prosperity, when there was an attitude of cooperation, government programs such as new schools and hospitals flourished but money was needed to finance these improvements. Bonds were sold to the public and the stock and bonds markets provided the funds needed by corporations to produce these valuable improvements to people's lives. But taxes were cut for the wealthy just as wages stagnated; the economy slowed and more and more of our production was transferred overseas. The need for money by our corporations declined while the wealth of the rich exploded. Industry, the basis of our economy, could no longer put the increased wealth of the rich to proper use, so more and more of the nation's wealth was directed to gambling in the stock and bond markets, and less and less on our infrastructure, education, jobs, universal health care and addressing planetary pollution. The financial meltdown followed.

We avoided a depression by rescuing the very financial institutions that had created the problem. But we failed to address the major cause of the problem.

THE MAJOR CAUSE OF THE PROBLEM IS THE CONCENTRATION OF MORE AND MORE OF THE WEALTH OF THE NATION INTO THE HANDS OF FEWER AND FEWER OF OUR PEOPLE.

As in many other areas of our society, it will be difficult to get back to the system we had during the period of Great Prosperity, when the wealthy did not gamble with their surplus of cash and those who invested in the markets did so primarily for the dividends and the long term gain on their stock.

Gambling can be addictive, and, like alcoholism, a problem to individuals, families and even nations. Resources that are needed for other purposes are squandered by gambling; we cannot deny that this applies to our nation as well as to individuals.

If we are going to make the investments needed to restore our crumbling infrastructure, convert to non-polluting energy, and return to the Great Prosperity, we need the money now wasted on gambling to bring about the conversion.

TOGETHER WE CAN turn Wall Street and the Markets from being giant gambling casinos back to helping finance the needs of the nation.

Chapter 15

FINANCE AND BANKING

*TOGTHER WE CAN turn our major banks into institutions
that serve the nation, rather than continue to be
monstrous gambling casinos.*

*"I believe that banking and institutions are more danger-
ous to our liberties than standing armies. If the American
people ever allow private banks to control the issue of
their currency, first by inflation, then by deflation, the
banks and corporations that will grow up around the
banks will deprive the people of all prosperity until their
children wake up homeless on the continent their fathers
conquered"*

~ Thomas Jefferson

*"And Jesus entered the temple and cast out all those who
were buying and selling in the temple, and overturned
the tables of the moneychangers and the seats of those
who were selling doves. And He said to them, "It is written, 'my house shall be called a house of prayer'; but you
are making it a robbers' den."*

~ Matthew 21: 12-13.

It is most unfortunate that humans as patriots and spiritual
people have not heeded the words of Thomas Jefferson and Jesus
Christ as we have developed our major banking and financial systems. Greed and selfishness cause us trouble almost everywhere in
our lives but nowhere are they more problematic than in our major
banks and financial institutions.

It started when some humans were able to accumulate more money than they needed. They began to make loans of their extra money to others who needed it. These borrowers then had to pay the original amount at a specified time plus what came to be called interest. Since those who wanted to make loans did not always know who wanted them and since those who borrowed did not always know to whom to go for a loan, banks were formed. Lenders deposited their money in the banks and were paid interest by the banks. The banks then lent it to borrowers at interest rates higher than what the bank paid the depositors; and kept the difference.

While I served in Congress in the 70s and 80s agricultural land values increased year after year. Then farm income declined along with land values. Farmers who had borrowed heavily using the value of their land as collateral were often unable to make their mortgage payments and as a consequence some banks failed. They failed because they made loans based on the supposed value of the land rather than the ability of the farmer to pay.

It should have been a lesson. It was not.

Banks serve an important function in a capitalistic society. They are part of a system that makes the society function and progress - giving people the ability to purchase property, secure education, set aside money for the future, pay workers and obtain consumer goods.

If I had not been able to borrow from a bank the money needed to fill the orders I had, Berkley and Company would never have even begun.

The trouble is not with our local banks in which people deposit money to earn interest, and others borrow that money when it is needed. The trouble comes from giant investment banks that underwrite and trade securities.

The current catastrophe and near meltdown of the world financial system demonstrates the problem of putting greedy humans in charge of other people's money. And there were both warnings and precedents in recent history.

With the collapse of the United States banking system during the Great Depression in the early part of the last century, federal laws were enacted separating banks into two types--commercial banks that took in deposits and made loans; and investment banks, which also took in money but were allowed to underwrite and trade securities. The law required that deposits in commercial banks be government insured and the banks were quite tightly regulated. In 1999, under lobbying pressure from bankers, Congress repealed the laws separating the two types of banks, enabling commercial banks to engage in the same risky practices as investment banks.

Repeal was a terrible mistake. It removed one of the comparatively safe places for humans to put their money. And it opened the whole financial system up to the gambling practices that ultimately came close to bringing down the whole world economy.

By nature, humans like to be free of government regulations and, indeed, some government regulations are pretty ridiculous. But there are areas in a capitalistic society where government regulation is a necessity.

The financial sector is one of them.

Banks serve a public interest by being a source of money to those who need loans and by enabling those with money to lend to earn interest.

Unfortunately in a capitalistic society profits tend to trump service to the public - this is more and more true all the time. In 2007, 26 percent of the United States economy's total profits went to financial institutions; this is four times the 1948 total during the period of the Great Prosperity.

It is difficult to see how the contribution of the financial sector to the nation increased to any great extent during the subsequent period of financial inequality. Financiers were simply finding additional ways to siphon off more of the money that passed through their hands while the government regulators stood by and watched.

The problem is that as we take more and more of the wealth out of the hands of regular people and concentrate it in the hands of the top ten percent, that money usually ceases to help the economy. And as the search by the wealthy for ways to become even wealthier continues, two possibilities arise, both of which further hurt the economy.

One is to get the government to reduce their taxes. With their political contributions and their lobbyist they have been successful with this beyond their wildest dreams.

The second is by gambling with their money. Here the banks and financial institutions, together with the commodities and stock markets have come up with all kinds of creative ways to gamble and stack the cards in favor of the gamblers. So we had hedge fund managers making billion dollar incomes, doing the gambling for the rich with all kinds of financial bets created by banks. When the bets went sour, the result was inevitable. Banks insured by insurers that did not have the money to cover investors' losses were bailed out by the government, with taxes paid by all the rest of us.

Our economic and tax system that enables the wealthy to accumulate unbelievable wealth is a disaster to the nation but Thomas Jefferson was correct about the problems with our banking system.

If a bank pays a depositor three percent on $100,000, and then lends that $100,000 at five percent it is easily seen that the bank makes a two percent or $2,000 profit (less overhead); if the bank would then borrow another $200,000 at three percent and lend it at five percent it would make another $4,000 and triple its profit.

When greedy human bank executives of the major banks realized and were allowed to do this, they didn't just lend three times their capital. They borrowed and made loans of 30 times their capital, a practice authorized by a federal government bent upon deregulation. The trouble is that this at first tripled and then by 30 times increased the risk that some of the borrowers would not be able to pay back the loans.

The primary goal of financial institutions was to make money and they began to invent all sorts of ways to do so. One of the most significant inventions was bundling mortgages and selling the bundles to other investors at a profit. Banks often retained some of these bundles because they liked the high interest rate.

Since the mortgage bundles included many mortgages little attention was paid to the ability of each individual borrower to pay the interest and principal.

This was so profitable to the banks that they started to bundle all sorts of loans, including credit card and automobile loans. And all the time no one was looking very closely at the ability of the borrowers to pay.

The banks then invented a multitude of derivatives of financial instruments including credit default swaps, interest rate swaps, interest only bonds, principal only bonds, shorts, short squeezes, to name a few. The important thing to know is that most of these inventions are meant to enable people to gamble in different ways and to cause them to believe that their investment is insured. Of course, the goal of the bank is to make money from each transaction.

For many years home ownership was an American's most significant and rewarding financial undertaking.

Well-meaning politicians saw this happening and believed home ownership was one way to help bring people out of poverty. Laws were passed that encouraged home loan institutions to grant mortgages. The motives were good - the results were disastrous.

Two government chartered entities were formed; Fannie May, and Freddie Mac. These were quasi-public entities that either bought mortgages and held them or packaged and sold them to others. Their purpose was to encourage home ownership. At one time they owned or insured half of America's $12 trillion in mortgages.

In the meantime rating organizations sprang up to rate financial instruments so that purchasers could have some confidence in the value and safety of their investments in bonds. There are three major rating agencies: Fitch, Moody's and Standard and Poor's. Like most business organizations in a capitalistic society, their goal is to make money. To make money, they compete with each other to get banks to use their services. A bank was more likely to use their services the higher they rated its bonds or packages of bonds. Sometimes staffing of the rating organizations was inadequate in terms of both number and experience.

Competing rating agencies frequently rated the bundles of mortgages with unknown or lower value at the highest possible rating[7]. What person would purchase safe treasury bonds, for example, at a low interest rate, when a top rated mortgage bundle of bonds was available bearing significantly higher interest rates?

To further complicate the matter, insurance companies saw an opportunity to make money by guaranteeing the mortgage bundles. American International Group (AIG) jumped into the market with both feet, insuring these bundles of mortgages and the different derivatives the banks had invented. Its hunger for greater profits, coupled with a lack of government oversight, meant that no one was looking at whether AIG had the capital to cover possible loss in bond value - it did not.

Let's go back to the individual interested in owning his or her own home. That person might have seen someone, like a neighbor, purchase a home for $150,000 that was now worth a million dollars and maybe at the same time seen a beautiful home for sale for $300,000. Maybe the person had an income of $30,000 per year. A mortgage salesperson would offer this individual a subprime mortgage with floating interest payments on which no payments would have to be made for one year and on which the first two years of interest would be below market but would escalate in the future. And all the while, in its continuing effort to encourage home ownership, the federal government continued its policy of allowing mortgage interest as a tax deduction.

Of course it sounded good to potential homebuyers. If home prices continued to escalate as they had for many, the buyer would end up with a huge profit and in the meantime live in a wonderful home. Never mind the possibility that the person could lose his or her job or that the value of the house might not continue to escalate. Or that once interest payments kicked in they might require up to half the buyer's total income.

At least temporarily the homeowner was happy.

---

[7] Fitch, and Standard and Poor's top ratings are labeled AAA; Moody's is Aaa.

The person who sold the mortgage received a commission on the sale and was happy. The mortgage was packaged with a number of similar mortgages and the issuer sold them as a package of mortgages for a profit and was happy. The rating company received a payment after giving the bundle an artificially high rating and was happy. The purchasers of the highly rated package of mortgages generating high interest rates were happy. AIG received a fee for insuring them and was happy. The banks, by leveraging at up to 30 to one, saw their profits and stock prices skyrocket; they made off like bandits and were happy. And the income of bank executives exploded to equal or surpass those of our athletic stars; they were *very* happy.

Ultimately, however, the whole thing finally came tumbling down when the persons at the bottom of the mountain, those with mortgage payments, were unable to make their payments and the trillions of dollars in financial instruments on which they were based went "poof"!

The banking industry had failed to recognize what my rural banks had learned way back in the 1980s - making loans without being sure of the borrower's ability to pay is a recipe for disaster.

To prevent a complete melt down of the world financial system (the failing bonds had been sold to purchasers around the world), the Bush and Obama administrations stepped in with taxpayer money to rescue AIG, along with Fanny Mae, Freddy Mac and other big investment banks. It can certainly be argued that the government had no choice if a worldwide depression, the likes of which had not been seen in some 70 years, was to be avoided.

The huge investment banks were considered by many to be "too big to fail".

But our federal government put the same people in charge of the policy making and regulatory system who had worked in the same banking industry that nearly brought down the whole world economy.

Unfortunately, but not surprisingly, things have not changed much. At one of the biggest banks, Goldman Sachs, executive bonuses are again on the rise as is Goldman's stock price. Even with its executives hauled before a Congressional committee, major reform at Goldman Sachs and elsewhere seems to await another near meltdown of the world's financial system.

If the banking system's greed can require a taxpayer bailout, surely the federal government must establish controls that protect against another such bailout.

It would not be difficult. The government needs to limit the amount of leverage that a financial institution can use. The commercial and investment banks need to again be separated. Commercial banks should only accept deposits and make loans. Since the depositor's funds are guaranteed up to certain amount by the federal government, they should be carefully audited. Investment banks need to be carefully audited and some exotic financial instruments banned. Insurance companies need to be required to have adequate reserves to make payment for losses. Regulators need to be given adequate personnel, funding and authority to make sure another meltdown never occurs.

In 1948, 8.3 percent of the profits in the U.S. economy came to the financial sector; 56 percent came to manufacturing. In 2007, the year the collapse began, the financial sector accounted for 26 percent of the profits; manufacturing produced only 10 percent of the profits.

We now need manufacturers to build non-polluting, more energy efficient cars to replace our fossil fueled gas-guzzlers. We need wind generators and non-polluting electric plants to replace our dirty coal burning plants. We do not need more gambling on credit default swaps and other risky schemes invented by financial institution managers.

When we look at solutions to national problems, we sometimes can find a state that has already developed a way out of the mess.

Way back in 1919, North Dakota created a state owned bank as a depository for all state tax revenue and fees; it still is in operation today. Its mission is to serve the people of North Dakota, not its managers!

North Dakota benefits from its energy and agricultural economy but one big thing that makes the state unique is its bank. As state after state finds itself in financial trouble, North Dakota has the lowest unemployment rate in the country and a budget surplus of more than $1 billion.

Since 1919 when radical reformers decided to start it, the Bank of North Dakota has plowed its earning into loans for the state's farmers, students and small businesspersons. And the bank puts half its profits into the state budget. It avoids the monstrous salaries and bonuses of traditional big banks because the governor serves as chair with a seven member advisory board of financial experts appointed by the governor.

The Bank of North Dakota has helped more than 100 private community banks and kept credit flowing to local businesses even while credit across the nation has tightened. Wall Street bankers do what is best for their executives and stockholders - the Bank of North Dakota does what is best for the citizens of the state.

No sensible person today would disagree with bringing millions of our citizens out of poverty; providing health care and education to all, and retooling our nation to eliminate burning fossil fuels. We can ill afford to squander 26 percent of the nation's corporate profits on financial institutions that pay unbelievable salaries to managers that spend much of their time promoting gambling schemes for the rich, when they should be concentrating on furnishing funds for building the nation.

If the $700 billion spent to rescue the big banks had been used to set up a national bank modeled on the one in North Dakota, and had that bank leveraged the investment at a modest 10 to one, we would have had $7 trillion in new lending capacity to jumpstart our economy with things such as helping the nation replace fossil fuel and putting people back to work in new ways to save our planet, rebuild our failing infrastructure and restore the Great Prosperity of the past.

This book is about the problems caused by a government that fails to recognize that REVENUE MATTERS; and a government that cuts taxes to the wealthy, and adopts policies that result in the concentration of the wealth of the nation in the hands of a small part of the population. It is hard to find a better example of the result of these policies than our nation's recent financial history.

TOGETHER WE CAN regulate our banking system so that it serves the nation through deposits and loans, not exotic gambling schemes.

Chapter 16

EDUCATION

*TOGETHER WE CAN do whatever is necessary
to make our educational system the best in the world.*

When I was a boy recently abandoned country schoolhouses dotted the countryside near my small hometown.

My grandmother and grandfather had attended one of them. Their parents were early settlers who did not have much in the way of luxuries but recognized the importance of giving their children an education.

Along with food, shelter and health care, education was and still is one of the most important components of a healthy society.

More and more research is confirming the value of pre-school education. It is not generally part of our public education system but is usually furnished by for-profit entities or by churches and other organizations as a public service. Not only do families have a place for their youngsters during working hours, the children jumpstart their learning. Since pre-school education is now recognized as important, it should be included in the public school system and be paid for by the taxpayers - and Head Start should be secure from budget cuts.

Primary and secondary education has long been recognized as extremely important to any nation. But in the United States today it is sometimes becoming a failure - particularly in the inner city public schools. The number of students receiving high school diplomas is less than 50 percent in cities like Baltimore, Indianapolis and Cleveland. Overall the United States graduation rate is about 70 percent; in Denmark and Japan it is well over 90 percent. Poland, the Czech Republic and Slovakia all do better than we do.

One of the problems with inner city schools is the current financial inequality that exists in our nation today. Our inequality is so immense that students in these schools have little incentive to study because they see little hope of having a financially rewarding life no matter how well they do in school. For the federal government to recognize that REVENUE MATTERS and bring back the Great Prosperity of the past would do more for our educational system than any other change we could make.

For a democratic and capitalistic society to function properly and for people to work together they must be educated. The deficiencies in our education system are therefore a serious problem to the proper functioning of our society.

We need to pay the money to get capable and proven administrators to lead the way in demanding improvement at failing inner city schools. We need to raise the pay of teachers and staff at all public schools, particularly those in our inner cities. If we want the brightest and best to be teaching our children, we need to pay them accordingly.

It is almost unbelievable that our Tea Party Republicans in state after state would cut funding for education and discharge teachers.

When things are not working in a business venture, one tries to find the problems and their causes, and correct them. We need to apply this to education and begin to try all conceivable approaches in primary and secondary public schools. When we find something that works we need to expand it.

Cost cannot be the issue. Education is sufficiently important that we cannot let the greed and combativeness of humans stop us from spending whatever is necessary to correct education's problems - and taxing ourselves sufficiently to cover the costs.

The G.I. bill for veterans has been recognized as one of the best government programs ever enacted. Today we need a universal bill like the GI Bill for everyone who graduates from high school.

In most of Europe higher education is not dependent upon family finances and should not be here in America if we are going to be a competitive nation in the world economy.

At this critical time in history our very survival depends upon the comprehensive and immediate action that solid education will bring.

TOGETHER WE CAN make our educational system the best in the world.

Chapter 17

HEALTH AND MEDICINE

TOGETHER WE CAN turn the creativity of our people loose to bring better health and treatments to the world.

As I write this I am 90 years old. Along with most of my older friends and almost anyone with health problems my health is one of my most important concerns. I am thankful for the wonderful care and treatment I have received after being hospitalized for various health issues.

In times past, tribes had medicine men who used various methods in trying to address the health problems of the members of their tribe. For ages humans used many different herbs and ointments as treatment.

But it is only relatively recently in the history of our species that our understanding of health and our bodies has exploded.

In 1847 Dr. Ignaz Semmelweis, known as the "savior of mothers," was ridiculed when he proposed that doctors scrub their hands with chlorinated lime in obstetrical clinics. His theories were not generally accepted until years after his death when Louis Pasteur confirmed that germs could cause illness. With the discovery that germs cause disease we started to look at health and medicine in a completely new way.

For several years, I served on The President's Council of the National Academy of Sciences

It was discovered that some germs could not survive in the presence of certain molds and penicillin was developed. This was followed by the birth of a new age of pharmaceutical drugs. The development of vaccines has pretty well eliminated the horrors of smallpox and polio.

When our first President, George Washington, became ill, he received the treatment of the day, which was to bleed him and administer mercury, one of the most poisonous materials known to man. It is likely he expired from the treatment rather than the disease.

Tremendous strides have been made in how we treat disease and maintain health. We have learned about the problems with smoking and the importance of good nutrition. Through dialysis and insulin injections we can help people with kidney problems and diabetes.

The list could go on and on, but we still have a serious problem - it is with the system.

There are two major problems with our current health care system:

One is how we pay for it. Allowing for profit insurance companies siphon off money for exorbitant payments to their executives and other expenses, is one of the reasons our health care costs are nearly double those of most industrial countries.

When President Obama tried to address the health care cost problem, the private insurance industry and other political contributors and their lobbyists succeeded in watering down the legislation to where it only partially addresses the problem - and it is being challenged in the courts as this is written. A single payer system, similar to that in place in many of the other industrial countries, was not even considered by the Congress.

Until we take out the influence of money in our government by passing public funding of Congressional campaigns, I see little hope of addressing our health care cost problem.

The second problem is the squelching of innovation in medical treatments. In most areas of our capitalistic society, competition in the market place determines what is purchased. Competition tends to hold down prices and encourages innovation. Our medical system, however, does not function this way.

The federal government, in its big brotherly effort to protect the public, adopted regulations that prohibit distribution of any medical drug until the Food and Drug Administration (FDA) certifies that it is safe and effective. This has created big problems including contributing to the explosion in the cost of health care - and it tends to stifle creativity.

The FDA does not conduct trials to determine whether or not a medication is safe and effective. Instead the agency depends upon the firm that proposes to market the medication to run the trials and furnish the data to the FDA. This costs the firm millions of dollars. It completely eliminates any non-patentable low cost medications from the market. What company is going to spend millions of dollars for permission to market a medication that cannot be patented and sold for a high enough price to get their investment back?

Most innovation comes not from giant laboratories, but from discoveries by practitioners and small operators who try doing things differently, and they find out it works. My fishing tackle business was successful primarily because we found a way to make a better fishing line. There was no government prohibition on our trying something new. Freedom to try things is what drives innovation - and Americans are highly creative.

In our nation's health care system, doctors are bound by a regulation called "standard of care", which is the accepted type of treatment for any disease. For a practitioner to try anything different from "standard of care" treatment risks the possible revocation of his or her license. It matters not how successful the new treatment may be.

It is proper for doctors to be prohibited from administering treatments that might be dangerous. But for doctors to be prohibited from administering non-toxic treatments that pose no threat to the patient, and with the patient's approval, especially if there is no effective conventional effective treatment is not in the interest of either the patient, or our health care system.

Because I believe alternative treatments cured my Lyme disease and prostate cancer several years ago, my wife and I have established a foundation, The Foundation for Alternative and Integrative Medicine (FAIM.org.) We are sending staff around the world to visit clinics and practitioners that are administering different treatments and we try to confirm their findings. We are shocked at what we are finding.

Senator Tom Harkin presents Berkley and Elinor Bedell with an award celebrating the fifth anniversary of their alternative medicine foundation. 2002

New discoveries of how our body functions and how to treat disease are exploding around the world. Since it was difficult to remove pharmaceutical drugs from reprocessed urine in space flights, electro-magnetic treatments were developed, primarily in Russia and other European countries. These treatments use the fact that each bodily organ, and each pathogen vibrate at a unique frequency. By measuring the strength of the patient's different frequencies, health problems can both be diagnosed and treated with the proper electro-magnetic frequency. Doctors in Peru were impressed by the improvement of patient's heart function with electro-magnetic treatments we took to them for trial.

Berkley with Dr. Gaston Naessens. I believe Dr. Naessens saved my life by curing my prostate cancer after conventional treatments did not seem to be working

Non-toxic medications are being used to treat many different diseases around the world. Those medications are low cost and cannot be patented, which makes them of no interest to our profit based medical system.

Stem cell clinics around the world are having significant success in treating all kinds of health problems. We have met with a heart disease patient who was told to get his affairs in order eight years ago, because there was nothing more conventional medicine could do for him. After stem cell treatments, he has lived a normal life for the full 8 years. We met with an MS patient who was having 20 seizures per day, and his family was starting to make arrangements for him to go to a nursing home. After stem cell treatment, he now lives a completely normal life and teaches golf. We have met with an airplane pilot who crashed his plane and was completely paralyzed from the waist down. After stem cell treatments, he now has regained all of his body functions; walks without a cane, and is flying once again.

All of these patients were treated in foreign clinics, because such treatments are illegal here in the U.S. Stem cell treatments are not "standard of care".

One of the major stem cell treatments consists of removing some of the patient's fat, bone marrow, or other body material and extracting the stem cells. The stem cells are then placed in some of the patient's own body fluid, where they will multiply, before being re-injected into the patient. There is danger to any operation, but there is no rejection of the patient's own stem cells, and the whole procedure is comparatively safe.

Can you imagine what it would do to our health care costs if heart transplants could be replaced by a simple injection of the patient's own stem cells --and what if we could take our MS patients out of the nursing homes?

After I retired from Congress, I worked with Senator Tom Daschle and his staff to fashion the Access to Medical Treatment Act. The act provided that any person should have the right to be treated by whatever treatment the patient desired, provided there was no evidence to indicate that the treatment would be of danger to the patient; provided the treatment was administered by a properly licensed practitioner under the limitations of his or her license; provided there had been no advertising of the treatment; and provided that the patient had signed a statement that he or she had been informed of all this and still wished to receive the treatment.

The bill was co-sponsored by both Republicans and Democrats, but we were never able to get it passed into law. What a heartbreaker! That law would have completely opened up our medical system to the creativity of practitioners.

Today in these great United States we have by far the most expensive health care system in the world. In most measures of effectiveness, such as life expectancy, we do not rate very high. We need to open up the system to the wonderful creativity of our people to take advantage of all the earth shaking new discoveries around the world in how our bodies function and how to treat health problems.

Reviving the Access to Medical Treatment Act is one way. There may be others. At 90, I have already lived longer than any of my former family members. If we will open up the system to the creativity of our people, I believe we will see an explosion of better science and treatments, and 90-year-olds will be both more common and healthier.

TOGETHER WE CAN bring the costs of our health care system under control, and open up the system to our great creativity to bring better health to our people and the world.

Chapter 18

ENERGY AND
PLANETARY POLLUTION

*TOGETHER WE CAN start taking steps
to end the pollution of the planet.*

"If you want to see an endangered species, get up and look in the mirror"

~ John Young, former astronaut

For thousands of years we humans existed on Earth without any concern for what we were doing to the planet itself.

Then we discovered that the shell of our planetary home contained minerals, including metals, coal, oil and natural gas, which had accumulated over millions of years.

We discovered that we could use some of the minerals to make wonderful cars, refrigerators, airplanes, ships, tanks, guns, and a host of other items. And we could use the coal, oil and natural gas for fuel to enable us to heat and cool our homes, travel in cars, trains, ships and airplanes and make all kinds of new materials, including plastics and synthetic fibers for clothing and other uses.

It was a new age. Combined with capitalism, minerals and fossil fuels literally changed the lives of humans on our planet.

Few thought much about what we were doing to our planetary home by robbing it of its minerals, burning hydrocarbons and polluting Earth's thin layer of atmosphere on which human life depends. Ultimately we explored the outer space around us and astronauts sent back pictures of this planetary home of ours. They were graphic illustrations of the fragility of our planet and the reality of our species being stuck here. People failed to realize the importance of this reality.

We humans have lived on this our planetary home for thousands of years. Our actions have not seriously threatened it - *until now*.

When I was born in 1921, we were one of the few families who owned an automobile. The ice man using his horse drawn wagon brought us ice harvested from the lake in the winter. We had no refrigerator, no television, certainly no Internet. Air travel was only a dream.

In the short span of my lifetime things have changed drastically. Most families have one or two cars, they zip across the country on a spectacular interstate highway system; almost everyone has a refrigerator, TV and many other electric appliances; air travel is an everyday thing; and the Internet has become one of mankind's most fantastic inventions.

It is wonderful but in the last few years we have come to realize that our planetary home can become unlivable unless we take care of it. But we humans have no place to move. Like it or not we are stuck on this planet. It is our only home and we ignore its health at our peril.

Just before I ran for Congress, I spent the night at the home of a friend on the seashore of Connecticut. That same night a former astronaut, Dr. Edgar Mitchell, was spending the night at that same home. The next morning he was out on the front lawn being filmed. As he sat beside a globe of the world, this is what he said.

> *"As we were traveling towards the moon in that little space ship with its limited space, limited resources, and limited waste disposal system we realized that we had to work together if we were to bring that flight through successfully.*
>
> *As I looked out that little window and saw that beautiful blue and white ball on a black velvety sky I realized that that blue and white ball we call earth was something special in this universe. It was home to living beings.*

Then all of a sudden a strange thing happened. All of a sudden, I realized that beautiful blue and white ball was a space ship just as surely as was the one on which we were travelling. It has limited space limited resources, and a limited waste disposal system, just as surely as did ours.

But whereas we were working together with our limited space, limited resources, and limited waste disposal system, the crew back there on earth was not doing the same."

Reprinted by permission

How right he was!

What if each of the astronauts had been judged primarily upon how much of the space ship he could take for himself to sell to others, or to consume himself? What if there had been no restrictions as to how much each of them could pollute the space ship?

When we sent astronauts into space, so that they could send us pictures of this space ship earth, it should have caused us to realize the vulnerability of this home from which there is no escape.

One of the problems is that there is a feedback in our atmospheric pollution. As the permafrost in the Arctic warms from climate change, the methane it contains escapes and pollutes the atmosphere. The effect of a ton of methane pollution on climate change is 30 times as damaging as a ton of carbon dioxide. The more methane that contaminates the atmosphere the more the planet warms and the more the permafrost melts; and more and more methane is released into the atmosphere.

Carbon dioxide itself is more than just an atmospheric problem. Oceans cover more of the surface of our planet than does land and we depend upon them for survival. Oceans absorb carbon dioxide from the atmosphere. Since the industrial revolution and the heavy use of fossil fuels, the acidity of the oceans has increased by 30 percent. Studies show that concentrations of carbon dioxide in sea water are going up at the same rate as in the atmosphere. The problem is that many of the marine organisms depend upon their calcium shells for survival. As the oceans become more and more acidic those shells are dissolved and that marine life disappears. Removing the calcium dependent marine life from our oceans threatens the whole cycle of marine life.

The population of zooplankton, the basis of the marine food chain, has dropped 73 percent in the last 50 years and the biomass of top marine predators is about one-tenth of what it was 50 years ago.

Rising sea levels caused by climate change are another problem. In the Pacific and Indian oceans nations such as the Maldives and Tuvalu have been forced to make contingency plans for the evacuation of their entire population due to the threat of the rising seas.

Half of humanity depends upon rivers fed by glaciers and ice fields. At the current rate of climate change, these glaciers and ice fields could disappear in just one lifetime.

The last time the U.S. seriously looked at our oil use was in 1975 when we passed the Corporate Average Fuel Economy (CAFÉ) standards for automobiles. In the next decade we cut our use of oil by 17 percent. Our imports from the Persian Gulf dropped by 87 Percent — in ten years. Most of that reduced usage came from automobiles that obtained more miles per gallon. Today we import 17 percent of our oil from the Persian Gulf Region. Just doing what we did in 1975 would completely eliminate our need for Persian Gulf Oil. Surely we can do better now.

I served in Congress during that entire 10 year period. The result of that reduction in the need for imported oil was to break the power of the Organization of the Petroleum Exporting Countries and for awhile bring back cheap oil. But once the price of oil moderated and the waiting lines at gasoline stations ended our concern over miles per gallon evaporated and government efforts to reduce oil consumption came to an end.

In fact, it could be argued that with the public's lack of concern, the lobbying power of the oil and automobile industries, and a previous president and vice-president with ties to the oil industry, our efforts to reduce oil consumption were reversed from 2001 to 2009.

Since recent events have shown that, left on their own, automobile buyers will buy heavier, more powerful, gas guzzler cars; there must be new government policies that will reduce oil usage and subsequent greenhouse gas emissions as we did in 1975.

My wife and I drive a Toyota Prius hybrid automobile that gets over 40 miles per gallon of gasoline in either highway or city driving. Technology is here for plug-in hybrid autos that bring still further improvement. With plug-in hybrids the owner could plug the car into an electric outlet when parked, which would charge the battery so that the car would use mostly electric power rather than liquid fuel for most of the travel especially on short trips. Commuters could plug their cars into an electric outlet at night to be charged with wind generated electricity while the electric load was at a minimum and drive back and forth to work using little or no liquid fuel.

I have consulted with Amory Lovins at his Rocky Mountain Institute. This institute is hired by industry to show firms how they can reduce costs by reducing energy use. Their clients include many of the largest firms in the nation. These firms have found that reducing energy use improves their profit as well as helping to solve a major problem of our society.

When I visited the Rocky Mountain Institute headquarters in Snowmass, Colorado, I saw that the building has almost no fuel costs and its normal electric bill is only about $5 per month yet its cost to build was only $1.50 per square foot more than typical construction. That $1.50 per square foot was paid back in only 10 months due to lower energy bills.

Current single pane windows are a major source of lost heat in most buildings. One of the improvements in the Snowmass building was replacing normal single pane windows with newly developed more efficient windows. Such windows in virtually any U.S. climate gain more winter heat than they lose, even facing north.

By using larger electric wires, better light bulbs, larger plumbing pipes, better windows and insulation, and other energy savings items, new homes can be built to use significantly less energy at very little additional cost.

The problem is that for most new construction, contractors bid on the project and the low cost bidder gets the contract without consideration of the economics of operating the building. If we are going to seriously take steps to solve our energy and climate change problems the government should mandate certain energy requirements for new buildings just as it does with CAFÉ standards for cars. And it could give tax credits and other incentives for retrofitting existing buildings.

Another way to attack the problem consists of replacing fossil fuels with non-polluting energy production. Here too the opportunities are tremendous.

When I was a boy, most Iowa farms had windmills to let the wind pump the water for the livestock. It was great to no longer have to pump water by hand. Then electricity came to the farms and windmills disappeared.

Today wind turbines to generate electricity again dot the landscape. Wind energy is non-polluting and there is enough wind to more than supply all of our electrical needs. One problem is that wind turbines only generate electricity when the wind is blowing but electricity from wind could be used to produce ammonia from water, which could be stored and used in fuel cells to produce electricity when the wind was not blowing. Such technology is not yet competitive with current coal generating plants but *we must not make today's economics an overreaching obstacle when our planet is threatened by current fossil fuel usage.*

We did not cut back the production of military equipment because of costs in winning World War II and the challenge we face with planetary pollution is equal to or greater than we faced in that big war.

Here is a comparison of the costs of various fuels used to produce electricity as reported by the California Energy Commission 1986 energy Status Report. These costs do not include subsidies or environmental costs.

Fuel	Levelized Costs (cents/kWh)
Coal	4.8 - 5.5
Natural Gas	3.9 - 4.4
Hydro	5.1 - 11.3
Biomass	5.8 - 11.6
Nuclear	11.1 - 14.5
Wind	4.0 - 6.0

Since 1996 the cost of natural gas has increased substantially and the cost of wind energy has declined slightly. Today the cost of non-polluting wind energy is already roughly the same as for highly polluting coal plants.

Two years ago wind generators were popping up like weeds around my Iowa birthplace. Construction has slowed and in some places stopped because the nationwide power grid is not capable of handling the new energy from wind.

TO POSTPONE CONVERTING FROM COAL TO WIND ENERGY BECAUSE WE DO NOT HAVE SUFFICIENT ELECTRICAL GRID CAPABILITY IS A DISASTER WHICH NEEDS IMMEDIATE GOVERNMENT ACTION!!

When I was in Congress I was a member of the alcohol fuels caucus. We were promoting the use of our excess corn production to produce ethanol fuel. With the increases in the price of oil, alcohol fuel plants were built across Iowa and the price of corn increased to where farmers could make a good profit from growing corn.

However, because of the cost of plants, the amount of energy used to grow and process corn into ethanol and the limited supply of corn, the contribution of ethanol to the energy problem is limited.

A large part of our electrical generation uses coal as the fuel. Coal is plentiful and cheap. Unfortunately, coal generating produces more carbon dioxide per kilowatt than any other process. It is claimed that technology makes it possible to inject the carbon dioxide from coal generating plants into the ground, but in 2011 the only coal plant sequestering carbon into the ground is a coal to gas plant in North Dakota - and it only sequesters 50 percent of its carbon dioxide.

We must solve the pollution problems if we are going to continue to use coal because one thing is certain. If we are going to seriously address the problem of planetary pollution we cannot continue to generate electricity from plants like the current coal fired polluters. As I write this we are still building the same old coal fired plants - what a disaster.

With the realization of the magnitude of the global pollution problem there has been a renewed interest in nuclear energy. At one time nuclear energy was projected to produce electricity at such a low cost that we would not even need to meter it. Such projections have not proven to be true; nuclear energy today costs more than double that of wind.

The potential for a nuclear holocaust is one of the greatest threats facing our human race. And the more uranium-fueled nuclear reactors that exist around the world, the greater the chance of diversion to the production of nuclear arms.

There have been no new nuclear reactors built in the U.S. in more than 30 years. Many believe that turning to nuclear energy would be like going from the frying pan into the fire and I tend to agree. I believe that there are better ways to solve our global pollution problem that should be tried first.

However we do need to find an answer to the nuclear waste that has already been accumulated.

My friends Ernst Bauer and Eleonora Anderson believe they have a process for the conversion of radioactive material into non-radioactive material. They have constructed a small plant in which they can demonstrate the process although conventional physicists maintain that it is impossible. If proven it would revolutionize our thinking in regard to nuclear physics and enable us to end forever the contamination of our planet by nuclear waste.

The process was developed based on work done many years ago in the mountains bordering Bavaria and Germany. There had been active silver mines in the area for several thousand years until about 10 years ago. They are now open as tourist attractions.

Processing the ore to recover precious metals was a local industry; each mine had its own experts who jealously guarded their recovery methods. The most common form of recovery in the small mines was based on black powder (gunpowder), which would generate high heat quickly and extract metals from finely ground ore. It had the added benefit of being cost efficient when working in small quantities. It fell out of favor when smelting processes became available and mines enlarged to mechanized production facilities.

The Lucich family settled in western United States in the early 1900s and brought the Bavarian process with them. Walter Lucich became a geologist and prospector. Together with Troy E. Becker and Janice M. Miller, he eventually prepared a report published in 1959, "Theory and Practice of the Lubec System of Metal Recovery from Complex Ores," that outlines but does not provide specifics about a proprietary method to recover metals.

My friends had a business removing pollution from contaminated ground such as closed gasoline filling stations. They learned of the Lubec process and its history, and hired a scientist to set up equipment to duplicate it. They found that it could not only extract precious metals from ores which appeared not to contain them but that it also could reduce and eliminate the radioactivity from radioactive materials.

They demonstrated the process in both Sweden and Italy. Highly qualified nuclear physicists witnessed it and the elimination of radioactivity of nuclear material was confirmed.

I recently met with a top nuclear expert in the U.S. Department of Energy. My request was that he send someone to visit these people so they could demonstrate their process and confirm that it works. I did not want anything else; all I wanted him to do was have someone *observe*.

I was greatly encouraged when he said that if they could do this it would be worthy of a Nobel Prize. You can imagine my surprise and shock when he later e-mailed me that he had consulted with other experts; they concluded that they did not believe it is possible and were not willing to even look! He suggested that my friends apply for a grant!

They do not want a grant. They do not want any money. They only want a chance to prove what they can do! As the expert said, it could merit a Nobel Prize and revolutionize our thinking in regard to nuclear physics.

The question is not whether these people can do what they claim. The question is whether we should be willing to overcome our skepticism and open our eyes and minds when someone questions current beliefs. Throughout the history of our human race such people have changed the course of our history.

We are on the verge of a global catastrophe from our pollution, but the pollution does not seriously affect the daily lives of most people. We cannot expect our people to make the necessary changes by themselves. Our federal government must be forced to take the steps leading to change.

We have a choice. We can continue current policies with elected officials serving the oil and automotive interests that help to finance political campaigns while ignoring the future potential disaster. Or we can elect leaders who will take the bold steps needed to build a brighter future for our children and grandchildren.

Measurements absolutely confirm that the amount of carbon dioxide in the atmosphere is increasing. Fossil fuels take carbon out of the ground and when burned, put carbon dioxide into the atmosphere. It is also clearly confirmed that the earth's climate is changing. The polar ice is melting; the snow and ice fields that furnish the water for rivers and streams that are critical to the lives of about half the world's people are going away.

It seems to me that the evidence is overwhelming but what if I am wrong? What if we convert all of our burning of oil to non-polluting energy sources and find out that there is no climate change problem?

Well, picture this; we will have removed our dependence upon foreign sources of energy and become self-sufficient, no longer dependent upon a finite source of fuel that is sure to run out eventually and an increasingly larger amount of which will be coming from nations that are not particularly friendly toward us. Climate change notwithstanding, it makes sense for us to replace imported oil with our own energy sources by putting many of our unemployed to work to do so.

Even neoconservatives should agree that properly addressing the problem of global pollution from fossil fuels is a win if I am right and a win if I am wrong.

When Henry Ford started building cars with a production line and started paying his workers wages that would enable them to buy those cars, he started an industry that has been a big contributor to employment, way of life and the economy of our nation. Today this domestic industry is threatened.

It is not that our workers are not adequately productive or that their wages are too high.[8] The problem is the system. During the recent financial meltdown the federal government pumped billions of dollars into the auto industry to keep the companies alive and preserve jobs. So what happened? The companies are now back advertising and selling cars some of which get about half the mileage of hybrid cars they are capable of producing. Obviously, if we are going to solve the global pollution and climate change problem - if we are going to push the automotive industry into the new reality - it is going to take governmental action.

Today many Americans can afford to drive big cars and heat and cool big houses. Most are not overly worried about climate change, the price of gasoline, or our dependence for oil on countries that are not that friendly towards us. The people who inhabit our planet are not going to take the steps that are needed to bring about the changes that we have to make. *It is up to the federal government.*

There are at least two recent lessons that should give us hope.

---

[8] Considering inflation, today's automobile factory workers are paid about half what they were at the middle of the last century

When we humans discovered that the ozone in the atmosphere that protects us from some of the harmful radiation from the sun was disappearing because of the release of the chemical chlorofluorocarbon (CFC) the chemical was outlawed internationally. The ozone layer is now replacing itself.

The bald eagle is the national bird and symbol of the United States of America. Dichlorodiphenyltrichloroethane (DDT) is a powerful synthetic pesticide that was widely used to control insects such as mosquitoes. But the widespread use of DDT was causing birds' eggs to become brittle and break, preventing the birds from reproducing. Eagles, in particular were almost wiped out. DDT was banned and today the bald eagle is no longer on the endangered species list.

In both cases it took worldwide government action to overcome the problem. It would never have been accomplished without governments requiring it. They were both global problems that could only be solved by global governmental action. Furthermore, economics did not drive the search for answers.

Let us look at one more reason for hope that is many times more significant. When I started to write this book, I had not talked with people at the Iowa Energy Center. I had no idea that there was a discovery that could be a major help in solving our pollution and climate change problem.

For a long time there has been an interest in hydrogen fuel because it burns clean and gives off no greenhouse gasses. The problem with hydrogen is that as a gas it is difficult to store and handle. Now, Iowa farmers and Iowa researchers are showing us an answer.

The farmers of our nation fertilize their fields with anhydrous ammonia (NH3), one atom of nitrogen and three atoms of hydrogen. In the U.S. 15 to 20 million tons of NH3 or NH3-based fertilizer per year are used in the nation's heartland.

There is no carbon in ammonia. Ammonia can be burned in such a way that it emits only water and harmless nitrogen gas (nitrogen already makes up 78 percent of our atmosphere). Ammonia can be produced from any raw energy source - wind, solar, nuclear, natural gas.

Today most of the ammonia used for fertilizer is produced from natural gas. Domestically we have more natural gas than oil. Natural gas is less carbon polluting than oil or coal but it still pollutes. To begin we could use the current ammonia plants to produce ammonia for fuel. They have extra capacity when not needed for the annual application of fertilizer. Then while we refit our automobiles we could look to other ways to produce ammonia. It can be produced from biomass or wind.

As we replace our coal-burning electric plants with wind-generated electricity we can have plants burning ammonia as a supplement when the wind is not blowing. That ammonia could be produced from wind-generated electricity produced when the wind was blowing, and stored for use when needed.

At this time we have an administration that is not controlled by the oil and gas interests. We have the recognition that our species is threatened by the burning of fossil fuel. And it appears we almost have a gift from heaven with a major part of the answer being NH3.

Ammonia is easy to liquefy and would be handled in a way similar to the way we handle gasoline. The current retail distribution method for gasoline could easily be converted to ammonia.

An ammonia pipeline from the Gulf of Mexico to Minnesota with branches to Ohio and Texas has served the NH3 industry for several decades. More importantly, since ammonia can be shipped in mild steel pipelines, any natural gas or petroleum pipeline could be converted to carry NH3 with cost effectiveness. Almost two million miles of natural gas pipeline in the U.S. could be converted to carry NH3, making it readily available to nearly every community in the country.

Like other fuels, ammonia can cause fires if not handled properly. Ammonia gas is extremely toxic and care must be taken in handling it not to breathe its fumes. But our farmers have been safely using ammonia fertilizer in large quantities for many years.

Let's do it! It is time to immediately stop building gasoline guzzling automobiles and trucks and change to non-polluting electric cars and, where more range is required add non-polluting NH3 fuel cells to the electric cars.

The place to start is with the trucks that serve communities across America and there is an obvious answer - converting the U.S. postal service fleet to using batteries and ammonia fuel cells instead of gasoline. It can be done by the President without the bickering of a politically polarized Congress and it could start us on the way to a fossil-fuel-free environment

The things we are lacking are general recognition that the survival of our human race is threatened by pollution, and the commitment of our federal government to take the steps necessary to save humanity.

Overcoming our dependence on fossil fuels is a huge challenge. But just as we mobilized to win World War II and just as we worked together to outlaw CFCs and DDT there is no question that we can do it.

I write this book hoping that in some small way it might help jolt us into addressing this huge problem.

TOGETHER WE CAN eliminate the pollution of the planet from fossil fuels.

Chapter 19

MILITARY FOLLY

TOGETHER WE CAN bring our monstrous
military machine under control.

We spend almost as much on our military as the rest of the world combined!

In recent years the United States, although surrounded by oceans and friendly neighbors, has had more of our fine young soldiers killed and injured in wars than any other country. Ironically, none of those brave soldiers died defending our nation from military attack.

At the same time, with our giant military machine, we have killed more innocent civilians than has any other nation. There is no better way to make enemies of friends, and antagonists of allies, or to build up the strength and appeal of would be terrorists.

We must ask ourselves how long this folly will continue.

In 2009, the U. S. spent $607 billion on its military. China, the next biggest spender, was at an estimated $84.9 billion or less than 12 percent of the United States' total; Russia, number five in the world, spent $58.6 billion. At the time former President Bush named them as the "Axis of Evil", the aggregate military spending of North Korea, Iran and Iraq, was a mere $10.6 billion. And if the list of our so-called enemies also included Pakistan, Syria and Cuba they added only another $6 billion.

The United States per capita figure was $1,986 for every man, woman and child in the country. Japan has a population of 128,000,000 and spent $362 per person on its military. India with more than 1,065,000,000 citizens and the threat of conflict with its neighbors gets by on $28 per person.

We have at least 700 military bases spread around the globe; total deployment at the bases is 250,000 uniformed personnel and an equal number of civilian employees. There are 47,000 United States military personnel in Japan and 54,000 in Germany. Most are there because of World War II, which ended more than 60 years ago when we defeated the two countries. Neither of these countries poses a threat of any kind to us today.

As we go about developing more and more effective ways to kill humans, we continually look at the short-term benefits, not the long-term effects. Our brilliance in developing better killing hardware is strictly a short-term benefit.

The invention of atomic bombs enabled us to end World War II, but the subsequent proliferation of nuclear arms around the globe now threatens the very survival of our species. No one is safe on Earth while nuclear weapons exist. Everyone would be more secure if there were no nuclear weapons in the arsenal of any country or if there was no possibility of terrorists obtaining them. The very existence of these weapons is an invitation to catastrophe.

The invention and use of the drone bomb delivery systems we now have is perhaps the epitome of effective, if terrifying, killing machines. They fly in, unmanned, to drop bombs on specific targets, killing people without danger to the killers. We have them and others eventually will as well.

We have developed some pretty effective ways to kill each other but the more we have, the more we threaten our own survival on this planet with its limited space, limited resources and limited waste disposal system.

It is hard to believe that there are not more questions asked about the tremendous amount of our spending on the military. The first question must be: "What is the purpose of this massive spending?" Surely the huge military force is not necessary to protect us from invasion.

Twice in the last century we sent our troops to fight battles on the plains of Europe. We continue to build tanks, weapons and planes to fight a land war. But Europeans are not about to start another war.

And would any major industrial country attack us and in the process ruin its preeminent customer?

It often appears that our military planners[9] and spenders are anticipating a battlefield out of the past with artillery, tanks and infantry, or huge ship-to-ship naval encounters. But with the world's arsenal of nuclear weapons and current missile technology, fighting in these ways is almost inconceivable.

And certainly our experience in Iraq and Afghanistan has shown us that military might is not the answer to terrorism.

The more we maintain military bases all over the word and the more we throw our military weight around the world, the more we cause people to dislike us and the easier it is for terrorist organizations to recruit additional numbers to focus their activities on us.

I believe that the United States needs to take a leadership role in negotiating the elimination of nuclear arms on our planet, but it is not in our national interest to be considered the "police force" of the world. Most of the world's people today do not want foreign military policing them and telling them what to do. And for sure they do not want foreigners dropping bombs from unmanned drones on them and killing their children.

It will not be surprising if in the future more radicals become leaders of nations that conduct terrorist activities. Addressing that problem should be the challenge of the whole family of nations not just the United States military.

We need to ask ourselves, "Have our recent wars in Viet Nam, Iraq and Afghanistan benefited us and made us safer and do we want to continue to be the imperialistic policemen of the planet?"

I have a favorite saying, which is, "The example we set for others in the way we live our lives is more important than all the fame or honors we may receive." This is just as true for nations as it is for

---

[9] In a sign of hope, however, Secretary of Defense Robert Gates broke with many years of traditional planning when he said at a West Point speech on Feb. 25, 2011, "In my opinion, any future defense secretary who advises the president to again send a big American land army into Asia or into the Middle East or Africa should 'have his head examined,' as General MacArthur so delicately put it."

individuals. As we build more and better killing devices, we set an example that is not ignored by the rest of the world.

If our species is to survive on this spaceship Earth, Americans must support every opportunity to take steps towards survival by cutting back our giant military fighting machine (and its cost) and pledging that a major part of what remains be used in concert with and by the United Nations to maintain peace and harmony on our endangered planet.

It is a tremendous opportunity that should start with asking questions about the real purpose of our military monster and its gigantic expenditure. What a heartbreak it is that we accept quibbling and posturing from our leaders who at the same time seem unwilling to ask such questions.

But if they cannot, they must be replaced by those who will.

TOGETHER WE CAN demand that we cut back the giant military budget, and end the practice of starting wars around the planet.

Chapter 20

THE NUCLEAR THREAT

*TOGETHER WE MUST demand that our leaders
take steps to rid the planet of nuclear weapons.*

Time was when the strongest person with the biggest club could rule. Then came spears, bows and arrows, and eventually guns. Guns were the great equalizer. Brute strength no longer ruled; with a gun a small person could do just as much damage as a giant.

Over the years, nations with the largest armies have been able to inflict their will on their smaller and weaker neighbors. War was accepted and even glorified and the number of men under arms was the principal measure of military strength.

Then came nuclear bombs. Nuclear bombs and the systems to deliver them have given nations the ability to destroy each other regardless of the size of their armies.

Just as guns were the leveler between individuals, nuclear weapons are the leveler among nations. Any nation with nuclear bombs and the ability to deliver them can bring about unacceptable damage to any opponent regardless of the size of that nation's conventional army.

It was on August 6, 1945, that we reached a huge turning point, destined to change the history of our human species.

That day pilot Paul Tibbets on the Enola Gay sent the five-ton, "Little Boy" atomic bomb plummeting down on Hiroshima, Japan. Sgt. George "Bob" Carson, the plane's tail gunner looked at a sight more devastating than any ever seen before; *"It's like bubbling molasses down there...the mushroom is spreading out...fires are springing up everywhere...it's a peep into hell!"*

Co-pilot Robert C. Lewis later wrote, *"My God what have we done?"*

Three days later a second bomb was dropped, this time on Nagasaki. On the day of the blast between 45,000 and 83,000 Japanese were killed in Hiroshima and 30,000 to 40,000 in Nagasaki. Another 75,000 to 123,000 died within the next several months. The numbers are staggering, as is the fact that we cannot be more precise. Dropping the bombs was one of the biggest disasters in the history of the human race.

Many Americans were quick to realize the long-term consequences of the bombings. They asked, "If we used such a devastating weapon on a foe, what would prevent our enemies from using it on us?" For more than half a century people around the world have been debating the morality of creating and using nuclear weapons.

This is particularly true of those responsible for building the first bombs, many of whom opposed using them against Japan without advance warning. J. Robert Oppenheimer, credited as providing the guiding genius necessary to create the bomb, later refused a request by President Harry Truman to help build a hydrogen bomb that was thought to be necessary in 1949 to counter the nuclear threat of the Soviet Union.

James Frank was a Nobel Prize winner and senior physicist during the days of the bomb-building project. He and a group of fellow researchers at Chicago's Metallurgical Lab sent a letter to Truman's nuclear advisory panel urging restraint. The prophetic document focused on the impact of U.S. nuclear explosives on the postwar international situation. It said,

> *"If we consider international agreement on total prevention of nuclear warfare as a paramount objective and believe that it can be achieved, this kind of introduction of atomic weapons to the world may easily destroy our chances of success. Russia and even allied countries that bear less mistrust of our ways and intentions, as well as neutral countries may be deeply shocked.*

It may be difficult to persuade the world that a nation which is capable of secretly preparing and suddenly releasing a weapon as indiscriminate as the rocket bomb and a million times more destructive, is to be trusted in its proclaimed desire of having such weapons abolished by international agreement.

From this point of view, a demonstration of this new weapon might best be made before the eyes and representatives of all the United Nations on the desert or a barren island. The best possible atmosphere for the achievement of an international agreement would be achieved if America would say to the world, "You see what sort of weapon we had but did not use. We are ready to renounce its use in the future if other nations join us in this renunciation and agree to the establishment of an efficient international control."

Dr. Frank is now deceased

It was a step backwards in the evolution of our species when the warnings and concerns of renowned and intelligent scientists fell on deaf ears.

By the end of 1949 the Soviet Union had detonated its own atomic device using plans received from spies in the United States. The U.S. responded by developing a hydrogen bomb 800 times more powerful than Little Boy and within a year the Soviets also had a hydrogen bomb.

By 1990 there were more than 60,000 nuclear weapons on the face of the planet. China, France, Great Britain, India, Pakistan and undoubtedly Israel had joined the club. In 2011 world leaders are grappling with the prospect that Iran and North Korea are on the cusp of having bombs of their own.

Here's the problem - guns, cannons and non-nuclear bombs kill but they do not threaten the planet; but if enough nuclear bombs are exploded, most of us will die and Earth may become uninhabitable for anyone who does not.

Historically the major challenge of any government has been to protect its people against invasion of their land by a foreign enemy. To accomplish this, larger and larger armed forces were built.

The military threat from invading armies is not an issue for the U.S. today. Our threats come either from planes or missiles launched from afar or from small groups of terrorists. With potentially tragic consequences, these threats are compounded by the existence of nuclear weapons.

What would the world be like today if the planes that flew into the World Trade Centers and the Pentagon had been loaded with nuclear bombs? Of course we believe it would not be possible to board a commercial airliner in this country carrying nuclear bombs but there are plenty of places in the world within striking distance where bombs could be loaded on planes. And it was a long time ago that nations acquired the ability to target New York or Washington D.C. with missiles.

Along with other nations, the United States over the years has agreed to the non-proliferation of nuclear weapons, accepting that each member of the nuclear club would destroy its weapons and prevent acquisition by countries that did not already possess them.

This is exactly outlined in Article VI of the Nuclear Non-Proliferation Treaty (NPT) of 35 years ago. China, France, Great Britain, the Soviet Union and the United States agreed, and in 2000 renewed a pledge: "An unequivocal understanding... to accomplish the total elimination of (their) nuclear arsenals..."

But now additional countries are acquiring nuclear weapons and the U.S. has not only failed to eliminate them elsewhere but at home we are working on new and better ones. We are reluctant to recognize and acknowledge the magnitude of the danger.

The danger that nuclear material could be hijacked by rogue governments of non-nuclear nations or by terrorists will remain as long as plutonium, uranium and the bombs themselves remain stored in poorly protected buildings around the world. The United States provides money each year to help Russia dismantle the nuclear arsenal built up by the Soviet Union, but the pace is slow and in the meantime, nuclear material continues to be produced.

Another imposing threat is the fact that when the Cold War ended, thousands of persons with nuclear expertise and the skills to build bombs found themselves out of work or underpaid.

A sign of hope might be that the nuclear states have cut the worldwide stockpile of weapons from 65,000 in 1986 to 30,000 in 2010.

But a sign of despair might be the Doomsday Clock maintained by the Bulletin of Atomic Scientists. In February of 2002 the minute hand was moved from nine to seven minutes before midnight--midnight being doomsday. The setting was the same at which the clock debuted 55 years before. The 2002 move was the third time the clock moved forward since the end of the Cold War but even worse, in January of 2010 the clock read *six* minutes before midnight.

Actions of the United States have been a significant focus of the Bulletin. In 2002, as is true now, the organization's board found it disturbing that our government was choosing unilateral action against enemies rather than cooperative international diplomacy. There was also regret that the U.S. had backed away from the Anti-Ballistic Missile Treaty and that we seemed willing to thwart international agreements designed to constrain nuclear as well as chemical and biological weapons.

In a 2002 press release, the Bulletin's board said, "Moving the clock's hand ahead at this time reflects our growing concern that the international community has hit the 'snooze' button rather than responding to the alarm."

The stance of the United States government is baffling. Even if we accept that our own extreme self-interest should have precedence over all else, why would we not take steps to help bring about the elimination of nuclear weapons on the planet, including our own?

In 2011 North Korea and Iran appear to be openly pursuing nuclear weapons. For Iran the reason is twofold; first to prevent an invasion and second to wipe Israel off the map. And in Korea, Leader Kim Jong-Il claims as well that he needs nuclear weapons to deter attacks on his country. Leaders of both countries point to the pre-emptive attack by the U.S. on Iraq in the second Gulf War as validation for their positions.

They have a point. Would we have invaded Iraq if we had known that they had nuclear weapons and the ability, to deliver them in retaliation to New York City, Washington, D.C., or other American cities?

Non-nuclear nations see the NPT as being inherently unfair because it prevents countries that have signed onto it from pursuing nuclear weapons and although the treaty provides that the original nuclear powers commit to destroying their arsenals, there is no timetable; so far it is being done slower than a snail traveling around the world.

Dr. Mohamed ElBaradei, former executive director of the International Atomic Energy Agency, which is charged with enforcing the NPT, rightly argued in 2005 that until all weapons are wiped out additional countries will seek nuclear weapons of their own. He said, "As long as some countries place strategic reliance on nuclear weapons as a deterrent other countries will emulate them. We cannot delude ourselves into thinking otherwise."

Leaders in the United States have complicated things and inadvertently added credence to the argument waged by Vajpayee and others by sometimes refusing treaties the rest of the world seems ready to embrace, such as the Comprehensive Test Ban Treaty and the 1972 Anti-Ballistic Missile Treaty.

Our own government seems indifferent to eliminating all nuclear weapons in spite of polls that show that 84 percent of Americans would feel safer if they knew that no country, including the United States, possessed nuclear weapons. Only 12 percent feel more secure knowing that the U.S. and other countries have nuclear weapons.

Various world leaders have addressed this issue in earlier times. In his Atoms for Peace address to the United Nations in 1953, President Dwight D. Eisenhower pledged America's determination to help solve the fearful atomic dilemma - "To devote (this country's) entire heart and mind to find the way by which the miraculous inventiveness of man shall not be dedicated to his death, but consecrated to his life."

John F. Kennedy, seeking to break the logjam on nuclear disarmament, said, 'The world was not meant to be a prison in which man awaits his execution.'

Rajiv Gandhi, addressing the U.N. General Assembly on June 9, 1988, appealed, "Nuclear war will not mean the death of a hundred million people. Or even a thousand million. It will mean the extinction of four thousand million; the end of life as we know it on our planet earth. We come to the United Nations to seek your support. We seek your support to put a stop to this madness."

Ronald Reagan called for the abolishment of all nuclear weapons, which he considered to be "totally irrational, totally inhumane, good for nothing but killing, possibly destructive of life on earth and civilization." The Soviet Union's leader, Mikhail Gorbachev, shared this vision, which had also been expressed by previous American presidents.

Today the United States is by far the strongest military nation in the world. The people of our country place a high value on national defense. But we must ask, "What is our goal?" It would seem to me that the answer should be quite obvious. Our military goal should be to protect and defend our people now and in the future.

At this time our policy and that of the world is to prevent any additional countries from getting nuclear arms. It is a halfway measure with three fallacies.

First, how can we possibly believe that other nations will agree that we should possess nuclear weapons, but they should not have them - especially when we are the only ones to have ever used them and have a policy of possible first use of such weapons? Most nations want to protect their people and there is no deterrent to invasion comparable to a nuclear arsenal. Second, how can we trust that all of those countries that now own nuclear arms will never decide to use them against us? Third, the main threat to our security at this time comes from terrorists. As long as there are nuclear weapons anywhere the threat of terrorists obtaining them is real

There is only one policy if our goal is to protect our people.

We must propose to the United Nations a treaty requiring all nations to agree that none will add nuclear weapons to their arsenals and all those that now have nuclear weapons, including the United States will PROMPTLY destroy them, and that all nations pledge their military support and whatever other tools are necessary to enforce the treaty.

Each nation would agree to permit inspectors from the U.N. International Atomic Energy Agency free access to guarantee compliance. The treaty should provide that all nations agree to act in unison in case any nation is found to be acting contrary to the treaty.

Although the United Nations has not always been effective and individual nations are not ready for and certainly would resist world government, there are divisions of the United Nations that have proven they can be effective. Our proposing and supporting this treaty in the only forum now available would start a discussion of this matter. Its urgency is obvious; it must be accomplished for the preservation of our species.

Of all the things we need to do, this is one of the most important steps to be taken if our species is to continue in a better and safer world. The longer we wait the more nations will have joined the nuclear club and the harder it will be to obtain worldwide agreement.

President Barack Obama recently took steps to control our arsenal vis-à-vis Russia. But he was roundly criticized from those on the reactionary side of the political spectrum. Nevertheless he should persist in his efforts.

TOGETHER WE CAN demand that the strongest nation in the world take a step to move the Doomsday Clock backward and move the evolution of the human species forward! TOGETHER WE CAN lead the world in negotiating a nuclear free planet.

Chapter 21

BAD NEWS - GOOD NEWS

*TOGETHER WE CAN turn our bad news into good news
if we will just recognize that REVENUE MATTERS,
and return to government of, by, and for the people.*

As I have pointed out in this book, we have a host of problems. But we also have the capability to solve our problems no matter how large. The question is whether we will decide to "put our minds to it" before the problems get too large to be solved.

Here are some of the items on which there is bad news, and good news.

GOVERNANCE
The bad news is that because of the exploding costs of political campaigns, members of Congress are so dependent upon the campaign contributions of Corporations and the wealthy that we have government of, by, and for, the rich and powerful and their lobbyists.

The good news is that some states have already shown us the way by passing public funding of campaign laws. We need to and can elect legislators that will pass public funding of Congressional elections, and take the influence of money out of politics.

REVENUE
The bad news is that we cannot provide jobs for our people; rebuild our infrastructure and convert to non-polluting energy without properly taxing the wealthy and corporate America to get the revenue needed. But

almost all of our Republican members of Congress have signed a pledge not to raise any taxes, or close any tax loopholes no matter what is needed.

The good news is that we live in a democracy, where we can throw out all those cut back can't do Republicans and the few Democrats that have signed such a pledge at the next election, and elect legislators that will recognize that REVENUE MATTERS and charge forward to bring back the Great Prosperity we had when we properly taxed the rich and corporations.

U.S. POLITICS

The bad news is that extreme partisanship and negative campaigning cause our government to put partisan politics ahead of service to the nation.

The good news is that the population is getting more and more upset with the government and can vote to retire those members that refuse to work together to serve the people rather than the wealthy and their cooperate campaign contributors. We have an example of how government can put partisanship aside and serve the people as was done during World War ll and the period of the Great Prosperity.

THE BUDGET AND TAXES

The bad news is that following our budget surplus during the Presidency of President Clinton, two wars, and tax cuts aimed primarily to the wealthy have created a massive budget deficit and a tremendous federal debt.

The good news is that we have enough super rich citizens and giant corporations that can afford to be taxed sufficiently to wipe out the deficit, and provide whatever funds are needed to put our people back to work solving our global pollution problem and building another period of Great Prosperity.

THE SUPREME COURT

The bad news is that the current partisan Supreme Court voted in a 5 to 4 decision, with all 5 Republican appointees voting to change the law so that corporations can make political contributions, further eroding the political power of the people.

The good news is that corporations cannot yet vote and members of the Supreme Court do not live forever. The people can elect a President and Congress that will replace a partisan member with a non-partisan one when one of the five current Republican appointees retires.

STATE LEGISLATURES

The bad news is that an organization, the American Legislative Exchange Council (ALEC) consisting of a large number of members of state legislatures and corporate giants now meets to draft legislation favorable to those corporate giants. The legislative members then work to get such legislation introduced and passed in state legislatures giving us some state legislatures that serve their corporate contributors, instead of the people.

The good news is that almost all of the legislative members of ALEC are in one party (the Republicans) so voters know who to vote against if they want legislators that will represent the people, rather than corporate America.

VOTERS

The bad news is that democracy is not working very well in the U.S. as over 30% of the eligible voters do not bother to vote.

The good news is that those non-voters make up a block that can vote out the legislators that are tying up our nation with their pledge to not raise any taxes, or close any tax loopholes. All they have to do is to GO VOTE!

JOBS

The bad news is that nearly 10% of our people cannot find jobs.

The good news is that by properly taxing the wealthy, we could give the unemployed jobs rebuilding our infrastructure and converting our energy industry to non-polluting fuels.

We can also shorten our work week to 35 hours and take more vacations as do the Europeans. By doing so and sharing the work, we could spend more time with our families and live less stressful lives - and eliminate the unemployment problem.

POLARIZATION

The bad news is that our political system has become so polarized that it is almost impossible to properly tackle the problems of global pollution, inequality, and building a prosperous and caring society.

The good news is that we live in a democracy, where votes replace the need for violence to change the direction of a nation. When the 90 percent of the people come to realize what is happening to them, they will surely vote out the current Tea Party influenced Republicans and elect politicians who will work together for the people.

FINANCE AND BANKING

The bad news is that the financial sector now pulls more than twice the profits of our manufacturing sector out of the economy; pays its executives outlandish salaries; and nearly brought down the whole world economy with its emphasis on gambling.

The good news is that by properly regulating the banking system, and possibly following the example of North Dakota by forming a federally operated national bank, we could put the nation's giant banks' enormous profits and salaries back into the economy.

HEALTH AND MEDICINE

The bad news is that our cost of health care is about to bankrupt our country. We spend about twice as much per person on health care as other industrial countries and our health is no better than theirs.

The good news is that we can break the monopoly of the pharmaceutical medical monopoly and open our system up to new non-patentable treatments, including stem cells and other non-toxic treatments that are being used around the world. By doing so we can improve our health and get our costs under control.

THE TEA PARTY

The bad news is that when the billionaire Koch brothers funded the beginning of the tea party movement they succeeded in getting some people to vent their frustration by demanding lower taxes and less government, exactly what will cause further inequality and economic disaster.

The good news is that people are upset. The worst thing we could have now is a complacent public. Once people realize that the battle today is between the wealthiest 10% of the people, and the other 90%, we can get back to the times of the Great Prosperity.

AFGHANISTAN

The bad news is that we are in the 10th year of a war in Afghanistan, which is killing increasing numbers of our own soldiers and large numbers of the people in Afghanistan and Pakistan - and appears no closer to ending than it did ten years ago.

The good news is that whenever we decide to do so, we can declare victory and come home. Al Qaida, the group that blew up the twin towers in New York, has already been nearly eliminated. It is estimated that they number fewer than 200 in Afghanistan. Osama bin Laden is dead. The Taliban whom we are fighting pose no threat to us. After our losing the war in Viet Nam, the Vietnamese people took over-- Viet Nam is thriving and is our friend. Continuing to drop bombs on Afghanistan and killing innocent civilians along with the Taliban increases the tendency of combative humans to hate us and become terrorists.

TERRORISM

The bad news is that a new threat called terrorism has come upon the world, where humans are willing to give up their lives to cause havoc among those whom they dislike.

The good news is that terrorism does not threaten national sovereignty as does war, and terrorism sends us a message that we need to learn to live together and not threaten each other. The best way to combat terrorism is not to threaten others so that they have more reason to hate us and want to harm us. It is a lesson we must learn if we are to survive together on this crowded planet.

MILITARY FOLLY

The bad news is that today, the United States uses almost as much of our wealth on the military as all the rest of the world combined - often only serving to make the rest of the world dislike us as we use it to unilaterally throw our weight around the planet.

The good news is that our nation is not threatened by invasion as are some nations, and Europe has shown us that war is not mandatory. We can bring back our troops from all over the world, including the more than 700 worldwide bases; cut the military budget in half; and have the money to do the things we need to do to bring back the Great Prosperity of the post World War ll society.

THE NUCLEAR THREAT

The bad news is that the United States, the most powerful nation on our planet, created a weapon that threatens the survival of our species - -and more and more nations are acquiring such weapons.

The good news is that as the most powerful nation on the planet, we can lead the way for all nations, including ourselves, to eliminate all such weapons and remove one of the major threats to the survival of our species.

PLANETARY POLLUTION

The bad news is that the burning of fossil fuels and the resulting increase in the carbon dioxide in the atmosphere and oceans threatens the ability of our wonderful planetary home to continue to support human life.

The good news is that we have both the resources and the technology to replace fossil fuels. All we have to do is recognize that REVENUE MATTERS, properly tax the wealthy and corporate America and with the proceeds put our unemployed to work in converting to non-fossil fuels-- and by so doing solve the unemployment problem and create the Great Prosperity we had after World War ll.

TOGETHER WE CAN change the Bad News in today's newspapers to the Good News we are capable of creating.

Chapter 22

SUMMARY

TOGETHER WE CAN .... turn our nation around.

As you have nearly come to the end of this book—and as I have probably nearly come to the end of my life here on this wonderful planet I thank you for considering my message.

As both a former business person, and politician, I cry for our great nation - and for the good people that make up 90% of our population but are asked to survive on only 18% or the nation's wealth.

> I cry even more for the 60% of our people that are expected to make it on only 7% of the nation's wealth.
>
> I cry for our planetary home, which we threaten to destroy with either our nuclear arsenals, or our planetary pollution.
>
> I cry for this great United States of America where we once worked together to win a big war, followed by a period of Great Prosperity, that has now lost its way with tax cuts for the wealthy and job cuts for the masses.
>
> I even cry for that top 1% of our people who own nearly half the wealth of our nation (42%). Many of them do not seem to realize how much better a society we would have if they were to be taxed sufficiently to bring back the Great Prosperity that once existed in our great nation.
>
> I cry for the Tea Party members, whom I believe care about our nation, but do not know what they are doing to our nation, and the Republican Party.

I cry for our non-functional political system in which the Republican party of Theodore Roosevelt, and the Republicans I served with in Congress have now let the Tea Party activists take over that formerly great party and turn it into a CAN'T DO, CUT BACK party that threatens the health of our whole nation with their failure to recognize that REVENUE MATTERS.

TOGETHER WE CAN turn our nation around.

Chapter 23

DREAMS

TOGETHER WE CAN dream of what we want
and make our dreams come true.

In this book I highlight the many ways we now threaten our very existence by the pollution of the planet, and the proliferation of nuclear arms. I highlight how our financial inequality adversely affects the lives of our people; and how our government has become unable to function due to the influence of money, and the pledges not to raise any taxes.

As part of the wealthy 10%, my wife and I would welcome the opportunity to give more of our wealth to save the planet for our great grandchildren now being born. If we all did it, it would bring great satisfaction to all of us, and none of us would have to deprive ourselves because of what we had done.

If it is to succeed it needs to be a team effort, a new team of Americans who care about each other and the future of our nation—with a government that represents the people rather than their campaign contributors—and everyone has health care, free education, opportunity for a decent job, and free time to be with their family.

I have mentioned this proposal to some of my personal friends. They laugh at me and tell me I am a dreamer.

They are right. I am a dreamer. I dream of my youth when we did not have today's inequality of wealth or today's political polarization, and we worked together as a team to win a big war. I dream of the nation we could be if we used the great wealth of the wealthy and corporate America to charge forward to build the wonderful nation we are capable of being.

The issue is what our dreams will be; the nightmare of a polluted planet that can no longer sustain human life; the nightmare of a nuclear holocaust; the nightmare of a nation where most all of our wealth is concentrated in the hands of a few, with millions struggling to just make it; or the dream of a species that has learned to live together on this fragile planet where we care about each other and about our planetary home--where our great wealth has been used to improve the lives of all of our people, not just a few at the top.

My dreams are clear. I hope others may share them - and take the steps to bring them about. IT IS UP TO US.

BERKLEY BEDELL

Berkley Bedell was born in 1921 in the bedroom of his grandparents' Northwest Iowa home.

As a 15 year old High School student, he started a business of making and selling fishing tackle with $50 saved from his newspaper route. That business became the largest fishing tackle manufacturing company in the nation.

After volunteering for service in the Army Air Corps he served by instructing young men how to fly during World War ll.

Berkley was recognized as the first National Small Business Person of the year in 1964 by President Lyndon Johnson at a ceremony on the White House lawn.

In 1972 he became disillusioned with the Viet Nam War. When his

Berkley and Elinor Bedell on their half of a 120 acre farm which they donated to the State of Iowa for the Elinor Bedell State Park.

The Elinor Bedell State Park was the first new State Park in Iowa in 20 years. The land included about 1/3 of a mile of shore line and was appraised at $1.3 million.

Congressman refused to listen to his concerns, he ran for Congress as a Democrat without any political experience in an overwhelmingly Republican district in Northwest Iowa. He surprised nearly everyone by winning 49% of the vote, and two years later was elected to the United States Congress, where he served for 12 years always winning by some 60% of the vote after his first election.

He was one of only a few members of Congress with business experience.

He left Congress because he contracted Lyme disease, and shortly after his retirement he was diagnosed with prostate cancer. Berkley believes both of these health problems were solved with alternative medical treatments. As a result, he and his wife have formed the Foundation for Alternative and Integrative Medicine (FAIM.org). This Foundation, run by their daughter Joanne Quinn, PhD, is searching the world for better science and treatments for disease. Berkley believes what they are finding will revolutionize how we treat disease and will bring better health to the world.

Berkley Bedell, with help from Jim Frost, has now written this book outlining what he has come to believe as a result of his 90 years of active life on our planet.

Berkley believes that our nation and, indeed, our whole civilization is threatened unless we change our ways.

JIM FROST

James G. Frost is an editor and freelance writer who has been working with Berkley Bedell on a Weblog and this book for several years. He first met Berkley while he was doing a consulting project for the Iowa Great Lakes Maritime Museum and the Arnolds Park Amusement Park near Berkley's home in Spirit Lake, Iowa.

He was in the event management business most of his life as chief of staff at the Minnesota State Fair in St. Paul; secretary/manager of the Clay County Fair in Spencer, Iowa; general manager of Minnesota's Dakota County Fair in Farmington, and executive director at Arnolds Park Iowa amusement park, now named Historic Arnolds Park, Inc.

He has also served as a consultant or project manager for the Development Corporation of Austin, Austin, Minnesota; Mission Creek theme Park, in Hinckley Minnesota; Northern Star Council, Boy Scouts of America, in St. Paul Minnesota; Thomas Carnival, Inc. in Austin, Texas; and VEE Corporation, in Minneapolis, Minnesota.

Jim has been an English teacher in Japan and a K-12 substitute teacher in Wisconsin. He graduated from the University of Minnesota with an English major and journalism and political science minors.

Working with Berkley Bedell for him has been fulfillment of a lifelong desire to take a part in expressing how he feels about social and political issues.

ORDER FORM

Phase V of S.W. Florida
12290 Treeline Avenue
Fort Myers, FL 33913

I enclose $ _____ for which please send me

_____ copies of "Revenue Matters" @ $14.75 each plus $5.25

postage. (The total postage of only $5.25 applies no matter how many

books are ordered.)

Name:_____

Address:_____

_____

Telephone: _____

Books can also be ordered from Amazon.com.

Berkley Bedell can be reached at:
Summer:	**Winter:**
15712 Rusty Road	160 Moorings Park Dr. #J-506
Spirit Lake, Iowa 51360	Naples, Florida 34105
(712)336-5070	(239)261-8398
berkley.bedell@gmail.com	berkley.bedell@gmail.com